Recipes

W9-CSL-617

American Cooking: The Great West

Contents

Introductory Notes 2
Appetizers and First Courses 4
Soups 15
Salads and Dressings 22
Vegetables and Garnishes 30
Seafood 43
Poultry and Game Birds 56
Meats 66
Breads 80
Desserts and Pastries 87
Mexican-American Dishes 113
Sourdough Cookery 136
Sources for Foods and Utensils 150
Recipe Index 151

Illustrations:
How to Prepare an Artichoke Bottom 17
Stuffed Flounder 49
How to Make an Icing Rose 96
How to Fill and Shape a Green Corn Tamale 117
How to Use a Taco Maker 121
How to Fill and Shape a *Flauta* 123
How to Fill and Roll an *Enchilada de Jocoque* 125
How to Shape a *Chimichango Dulce* 129
San Francisco Sourdough Bread 144

Foods of the World

TIME-LIFE BOOKS, NEW YORK

Introductory Notes

Techniques for Home Canning

To ensure consistent results in home canning, use standard canning jars or jelly glasses with matching lids. Examine each jar or glass carefully and discard those with covers that do not fit securely and those with cracked or chipped edges. An airtight seal is essential to prevent spoilage.

Wash the jars, glasses, lids and rings in hot, soapy water and rinse them with scalding water. Place them in a large deep pot and pour in enough hot water to cover them completely. Bring to a boil over high heat, then turn off the heat and let the pot stand while you finish cooking the food that you plan to can. The jars or glasses must be hot when the food is placed in them.

(If you have a dishwasher with a sanitizing cycle, simply run the jars, glasses, lids and rings through the cycle, using your usual detergent. Leave them in the closed machine until you are ready to can.)

To prepare for sealing the glasses, grate a 4-ounce bar of paraffin into the top of a double boiler (preferably one with a pouring spout) and melt it over hot water. Do not let the paraffin get so hot that it begins to smoke; it can catch fire easily.

When the food is ready for canning, lift the jars or glasses from the pot with tongs and stand them upright on a level surface. Leave the lids and rings in the pot until you are ready to use them. Fill and seal the jars one at a time, filling each jar to within ⅛ inch of the top and each glass to within ½ inch of the top. Each jar should be sealed quickly and tightly with its ring and lid.

The jelly glasses also should be sealed at once. Pour a single thin layer of hot paraffin over the surface of the jelly, making sure it covers the jelly completely and touches all sides of the glass. If air bubbles appear in the paraffin, prick them immediately with the tip of a knife. Let the paraffin cool and harden; then cover the glasses with metal lids.

NOTE: If there is not enough food to fill the last jar or glass completely, do not seal it; refrigerate and use the food as soon as possible.

How to Handle Hot Chilies

Hot peppers, or chilies, vary in piquancy—sometimes even on a single plant. The fresh red and green chilies used in recipes in this book are generally hot. (Fresh green chilies are underripe red chilies, and taste almost the same.) Canned green chilies are mildly piquant; canned *jalapeño* chilies are fiery. Though most dried chilies are hot, the *ancho* variety is almost sweet and is used primarily to give sauces a maroon color.

The volatile oils in any of these chilies may burn your skin and make your eyes smart. Wear rubber gloves if you can, and be careful not to touch your face while working with chilies. After handling the hot peppers, wash your hands (and the gloves) thoroughly with soap and water.

Before chopping chilies, rinse them clean and pull out the stems under cold running water. Break or cut the pods in half and brush out the seeds. The chilies may be used at once or soaked in cold salted water for an hour or so to make them less hot.

Small dried chilies should be stemmed, broken open and seeded before they are used. Dried *ancho* chilies should be plumped as well. Place the seeded *ancho* chilies in a bowl, pour in enough boiling water to cover them completely, and let them soak for at least 30 minutes. If you wish to remove the skins, slip them off with your fingers or a small knife, or put the chilies through the finest blade of a food mill.

Canned chilies should always be rinsed in cold water (to remove the brine in which they were preserved) before they are cut and seeded.

APPETIZERS & FIRST COURSES

Texas Broiled Shrimp

To serve 4 to 6 as a first course or
  6 to 8 as an appetizer

1 pound uncooked medium-sized
  shrimp (about 20 to 24 to the
  pound)
1 cup vegetable oil
¼ cup strained fresh lemon juice

2 or 3 large garlic cloves, peeled
  and crushed with a kitchen mallet
  or the flat of a heavy cleaver
¼ cup finely chopped fresh parsley
Salt
Freshly ground black pepper

Shell the shrimp, leaving the tail and the last segment of shell intact. Devein the shrimp by making a shallow incision down their backs with a
small sharp knife and lifting out the black or white intestinal vein with
the point of the knife. Wash the shrimp under cold running water and
pat them completely dry with paper towels.

Combine the vegetable oil, lemon juice and garlic in a bowl and mix
well. Drop in the shrimp and turn them about with a spoon to coat them
evenly. Then cover the bowl tightly with aluminum foil or plastic wrap
and marinate the shrimp in the refrigerator for about 12 hours, turning
them over occasionally.

Immerse two dozen individual Oriental bamboo skewers in water and
soak them for at least an hour to prevent the skewers from charring when
the shrimp are broiled. Then light a layer of charcoal briquettes in a
hibachi and let them burn until a white ash appears on the surface. Or
preheat the broiler of the oven to its highest setting.

Remove the shrimp from the marinade and spear each one with a
skewer. Broil the shrimp about 4 inches from the heat for 2 to 3 minutes
on each side, or until they are delicately browned.

Arrange the skewered shrimp attractively on a heated platter and
sprinkle them with the chopped parsley. Season the shrimp lightly with
salt and a few grindings of pepper and serve at once.

Huevos Monterey
TORTILLAS BAKED WITH ARTICHOKE HEARTS AND CHEESE-TOPPED EGGS

To serve 4

8 teaspoons butter, softened
4 corn tortillas *(page 118)*,
   thoroughly defrosted if frozen
4 dried hot red chilies, each about
   1½ inches long, stemmed,
   seeded and coarsely crumbled
   (caution: see note, page 3)
2 medium-sized garlic cloves, peeled
   and coarsely chopped
2 teaspoons salt
A 1-pound 12-ounce can whole

tomatoes
1 teaspoon crumbled dried oregano
½ teaspoon ground cumin
A 10-ounce package frozen
   artichoke hearts, thoroughly
   defrosted, patted dry with paper
   towels, and sliced crosswise into
   ¼-inch-thick rounds
8 eggs
2 cups (½ pound) finely grated
   Monterey Jack cheese
1 cup finely chopped onions

Preheat the oven to 400°. With a pastry brush, spread 4 teaspoons of the softened butter evenly over the bottom of four heatproof serving plates or individual shallow baking dishes about 6 inches in diameter. Place a tortilla on each plate or dish and brush the tops with the remaining 4 teaspoons of softened butter. Set aside.

With a mortar and pestle, or in a small bowl with the back of a spoon, rub the chilies, garlic and salt to a smooth paste. Drain the tomatoes in a sieve set over a bowl and chop them coarsely.

Combine the chili-and-garlic paste, the tomatoes and their liquid, the oregano and the cumin in a heavy 10- to 12-inch skillet. Stirring constantly, bring to a boil over high heat. Then cook briskly, stirring from time to time, until the sauce is thick enough to hold its shape almost solidly in a spoon. Remove from the heat and taste the sauce for seasoning.

Arrange the sliced artichoke hearts in a ring around the outside edge of each tortilla. Pour the tomato sauce over the tortillas, masking the artichoke-heart rings completely. Break 2 eggs into the center of each ring and bake in the middle of the oven for 2 or 3 minutes. Then sprinkle each pair of eggs with ¼ cup of the cheese, and continue baking for 5 or 6 minutes longer, until the cheese has melted and the eggs are set.

Serve the *huevos Monterey* at once, directly from the baking dishes. Mound the chopped onions in a small bowl and present them separately as an accompaniment.

Cold Boiled Artichokes with Tuna Mayonnaise
To serve 4

ARTICHOKES
Four 12- to 14-ounce artichokes

1 lemon, cut in half
2 tablespoons salt

With a small sharp knife, trim the bases of the artichokes flush and flat. Bend and snap off the small bottom leaves and any bruised outer leaves. Lay each artichoke on its side, grip it firmly, and slice about 1 inch off the top. With scissors, trim ¼ inch off the points of the rest of the leaves, rubbing all the cut edges with lemon to prevent discoloring as you proceed. To remove the chokes, spread the top leaves apart with your fingers and twist out the inner core of thistlelike yellow leaves *(drawings, page 17)*. Then, with a long-handled spoon, scrape out the hairy chokes inside. Squeeze a little lemon juice into the cavity of each artichoke, then press the artichokes back into shape.

In a large enameled casserole or pot, bring 4 quarts of water and the 2 tablespoons of salt to a boil over high heat. Drop in the artichokes and return the water to a boil. Cook briskly, uncovered, for about 20 minutes, or until the artichoke bases show no resistance when pierced with the point of a small sharp knife.

With tongs, transfer the artichokes to a colander and invert them to drain. When they are cool enough to handle, arrange them upside down in a baking dish lined with paper towels and refrigerate them for at least 2 hours, or until they are thoroughly chilled.

Meanwhile, prepare the tuna mayonnaise.

TUNA MAYONNAISE
1½ cups vegetable oil
A 3-ounce can white tuna, drained
4 flat anchovy fillets, drained
3 egg yolks, at room temperature
1½ teaspoons dry mustard
¼ teaspoon ground hot red pepper

(cayenne)
¼ cup strained fresh lemon juice
2 tablespoons capers, drained,
rinsed in a sieve under cold
running water, and finely
chopped
Salt (optional)

Combine the vegetable oil, tuna and anchovies in the jar of an electric blender and blend at high speed for 30 seconds. Turn off the machine, scrape down the sides of the jar with a rubber spatula, and blend again until the mixture is a smooth purée.

Warm a large mixing bowl in hot water, dry it quickly but thoroughly, and drop in the egg yolks. With a wire whisk or a rotary or electric beater, beat the yolks vigorously for about 2 minutes, until they thicken and cling to the whisk or beater. Stir in the mustard and red pepper. Beat in about ½ cup of the tuna-oil purée, ½ teaspoon at a time; make sure each addition is absorbed before adding more. By the time ½ cup of the purée has been beaten in, the mayonnaise should have the consistency of very thick cream.

Beating constantly, pour in the remaining tuna-oil purée in a slow, thin stream. Stir in the lemon juice and capers, taste for seasoning and add salt if desired. Cover the bowl tightly with foil or plastic wrap and refrigerate until ready to use.

Just before serving, ladle about a tablespoonful of the tuna mayonnaise into the center of each artichoke and arrange the artichokes on a chilled platter. Spoon the rest of the tuna mayonnaise into a small bowl or sauceboat and present it separately with the artichokes.

Guacamole with Chilies
AVOCADO DIP

To make about 2 cups

2 large ripe avocados
1 large firm ripe tomato, peeled, seeded and finely chopped *(see chile con queso, page 8)*
2 hard-cooked eggs, finely chopped
½ cup finely chopped onions
2 canned green chilies (not the *jalapeño* variety), drained, seeded and finely chopped
1 tablespoon strained fresh lime juice
2 teaspoons salt
1 tablespoon finely chopped fresh coriander (optional)
Tostaditas (page 122)

Cut the avocados in half. With the tip of a small knife, loosen the seeds and lift them out. Remove any brown tissuelike fibers that cling to the flesh. Strip off the skins with your fingers or the knife, starting at the narrow or stem end. Chop the avocados coarsely; then, in a deep bowl, mash them to a rough purée. Add the tomato, half of the chopped eggs, the onions, chilies, lime juice and salt, and mix them together gently but thoroughly. Taste for seasoning.

Mound the *guacamole* in a serving bowl, scatter the remaining chopped eggs over it and, if you are using it, sprinkle the coriander on top. Serve at once, accompanied by the *tostaditas*.

Angelenos
ANGELS ON HORSEBACK, CALIFORNIA STYLE

To serve 6 to 8 as a first course

¼ cup strained fresh lemon juice
1 tablespoon Worcestershire sauce
1 tablespoon anchovy paste
2 dozen shucked oysters, thoroughly

defrosted if frozen
12 lean bacon slices, cut crosswise
in half
1 tablespoon vegetable oil

Combine the lemon juice, Worcestershire sauce and anchovy paste in a bowl and stir until the mixture is smooth. Pat the oysters completely dry with paper towels, then drop them into the mixture and turn them about with a spoon to coat them evenly. Let the oysters marinate at room temperature for about 1 hour.

Preheat the broiler to its highest setting. Remove the oysters from the marinade, wrap each one in a bacon half and run a wooden toothpick completely through the oyster to hold the bacon in place. With a pastry brush, spread the oil evenly over the broiler pan rack. Arrange the oysters in one layer on the rack and broil them 4 inches from the heat for about 2 minutes on each side, turning them with tongs. When the bacon is crisp and golden, arrange the *angelenos* attractively on a heated platter and serve them at once.

Chile con Queso
CHEESE-AND-GREEN-CHILI DIP

To make 2½ to 3 cups

3 medium-sized firm ripe tomatoes
  or 1 cup chopped drained canned
  tomatoes
2 tablespoons butter
2 tablespoons flour
1 cup light cream
½ teaspoon finely chopped garlic
½ teaspoon salt

A 4-ounce can green chilies (not
  the *jalapeño* variety), drained,
  stemmed, seeded and finely
  chopped
2 cups (½ pound) freshly grated
  Monterey Jack cheese, or
  substitute 2 cups freshly grated
  Münster cheese

If you are using fresh rather than canned tomatoes, drop them into enough boiling water to immerse them completely. After 15 seconds, run the tomatoes under cold water and peel them with a small sharp knife. Then cut out the stems, slice the tomatoes in half crosswise and squeeze the halves gently to remove the seeds and juice. Chop the tomatoes coarsely.

In a heavy 1- to 1½-quart saucepan, melt the butter over moderate heat. When the foam begins to subside, add the flour and mix well. Stirring constantly with a wire whisk, pour in the cream in a slow, thin stream and cook over high heat until the sauce comes to a boil, thickens heavily and is smooth. Reduce the heat to low and simmer for 2 or 3 minutes to remove any taste of raw flour. Set the sauce aside off the heat.

Combine the tomatoes, garlic and salt in a heavy 10- to 12-inch skillet and, stirring frequently, cook briskly, uncovered, until the mixture is thick enough to hold its shape almost solidly in a spoon. Reduce the heat to low and stir in the cream sauce and chilies. Without letting the mixture boil, stir in the grated cheese a handful at a time.

To serve, light the burner under a fondue pot or chafing dish. If you are using a chafing dish, pour hot (not boiling) water into the bottom pan. Ladle the *chile con queso* into the fondue pot or chafing dish and serve at once, accompanied by *tostaditas (page 122)* or crackers.

Crab-Olive Spread

To make about 2½ cups

½ cup homemade mayonnaise
(*page 29*), or substitute
½ cup unsweetened bottled
mayonnaise
2 tablespoons finely chopped fresh
parsley
2 teaspoons strained fresh lemon
juice

2 teaspoons Worcestershire sauce
1 teaspoon bottled horseradish
2 hard-cooked eggs, finely chopped
½ cup finely chopped ripe olives
1 cup freshly cooked, canned or
defrosted frozen crabmeat,
drained and picked over to
remove all bits of shell and
cartilage

Combine the mayonnaise, parsley, lemon juice, Worcestershire sauce and horseradish in a deep bowl and mix well. Stir in the chopped eggs and olives and, when they are thoroughly incorporated, gently fold in the crabmeat. Serve at once as a spread for crackers, or cover the bowl with plastic wrap and refrigerate until ready to serve. Tightly covered, the crab-olive spread can safely be kept in the refrigerator for a day.

Turcos

TINY DEEP-FRIED SPICED-BEEF TURNOVERS

To make about 10 dozen turnovers

PASTRY
6 cups unsifted flour
1½ teaspoons salt

1½ cups vegetable shortening, cut
into ½-inch bits
1 to 1¼ cups ice water

Turcos were probably named for their shape, which is reminiscent of the half-moon on the Turkish flag.

First prepare the pastry in the following manner: Combine the flour, 1½ teaspoons of salt and the shortening in a deep bowl and, with your fingertips, rub the flour and fat together until the mixture resembles flakes of coarse meal. Pour in 1 cup of the ice water all at once and mix with your fingers or a fork until the dough can be gathered into a compact ball. If the dough seems crumbly, add up to ¼ cup more ice water by the teaspoonful until the particles adhere. Wrap the dough in wax paper and refrigerate it for at least 1 hour.

FILLING
½ pound lean top round beef,
trimmed of excess fat
2 tablespoons lard
½ cup finely chopped onions
¼ cup finely chopped celery
1 teaspoon finely chopped garlic
3 medium-sized firm ripe tomatoes,
peeled, seeded and finely chopped
(see chile con queso, page 8)
½ cup finely chopped sweet green

bell peppers
1½ teaspoons sugar
½ teaspoon ground cumin
¼ teaspoon ground hot red pepper
(cayenne)
1 teaspoon salt
¼ cup finely chopped pecans
¼ cup finely chopped raisins

Vegetable oil for deep frying

Meanwhile, make the filling. Freeze the beef for 10 to 15 minutes, or until it is firm but not solidly frozen. With a large sharp knife, cut the beef into ⅛-inch-thick slices and then into ⅛-inch dice.

In a heavy 10- to 12-inch skillet, melt the lard over moderate heat until it is very hot but not smoking. Add the onions, celery and garlic and, stirring frequently, cook for about 5 minutes. When the vegetables are soft but not brown, stir in the diced beef, the tomatoes, bell peppers, sugar, cumin, red pepper and 1 teaspoon of salt. Stirring frequently, cook over moderate heat until almost all of the liquid in the pan has evaporated. Add the pecans and raisins, mix well, and taste for seasoning. Set the filling aside to cool to room temperature.

Cut off about one fourth of the pastry dough, shape it into a ball and return the rest to the refrigerator. On a lightly floured surface, roll the ball of dough into a rough circle about ⅛ inch thick. With a cookie cutter or the rim of a glass, cut the dough into 2½-inch rounds. Gather the scraps of dough into a ball, roll it out as before and cut as many more 2½-inch rounds as you can.

To shape each *turco,* moisten the edges of a pastry round with a finger dipped in cold water. Place 1 teaspoon of the filling in the center of the round and fold the two sides together to make a tiny half-moon-shaped turnover. Crimp the edges with your fingers or with the tines of a fork.

Repeat the procedure until all of the dough has been rolled, cut and shaped into turnovers. At this stage, the pastries may be wrapped in foil and refrigerated for a day or so, or frozen for up to three months.

To fry the *turcos,* pour vegetable oil into a deep fryer or large heavy saucepan to a depth of about 3 inches and heat the oil until it reaches a temperature of 375° on a deep-frying thermometer. Meanwhile, preheat the oven to its lowest setting. Line one or more jelly-roll pans with a double thickness of paper towels and place them in the oven.

Deep-fry four or five *turcos* at a time, turning them about with a slotted spoon for about 5 minutes, or until they are crisp and golden brown. As they color, transfer the *turcos* to the lined pan and keep them warm in the oven while you fry the rest.

Arrange the *turcos* on a heated platter and serve immediately.

Texas Caviar
PICKLED BLACK-EYED PEAS

To serve 10 to 12 as an
  accompaniment to drinks

5 cups water
2 cups (about 1 pound) dried black-
  eyed peas
3 teaspoons salt
¾ cup red wine vinegar
½ teaspoon freshly ground black
  pepper

2 cups olive oil
1 medium-sized onion, peeled, cut
  crosswise into ¼-inch-thick
  slices and separated into rings
2 large garlic cloves, peeled and
  bruised slightly with a kitchen
  mallet or the side of a heavy
  cleaver or knife
1 tablespoon finely chopped fresh
  parsley

In a heavy 3- to 4-quart saucepan, bring the water to a boil over high heat. Drop in the black-eyed peas and cook briskly for 2 minutes, then turn off the heat and let the peas soak for 1 hour. Add 1 teaspoon of the salt and bring the mixture to a boil again over high heat. Reduce the heat to low and simmer partially covered for 40 to 50 minutes, or until the peas are tender but still somewhat firm to the bite. Drain the peas in a sieve or colander and discard the cooking liquid.

Meanwhile, combine the vinegar, the remaining 2 teaspoons of salt and the pepper in a deep bowl and stir with a wire whisk until the salt dissolves. Whisking constantly, pour in the oil in a slow, thin stream and con-

Continued on next page

tinue to beat until the marinade mixture is thick and smooth.

Add the black-eyed peas, onion rings and garlic to the marinade, turning them about with a spoon to coat them evenly. Cover the bowl tightly with foil or plastic wrap and marinate in the refrigerator for 2 or 3 days, stirring the peas occasionally.

Before serving, pick out and discard the garlic cloves and taste the peas for seasoning. With a slotted spoon, transfer the peas and onion rings to a chilled serving bowl. Moisten the Texas caviar with a few spoonfuls of the marinade and scatter the parsley over the top. Serve the Texas caviar at once as an accompaniment to drinks.

Caraway Twists

To make about 4 dozen twists

	into ¼-inch bits
1½ cups unsifted flour	2 tablespoons vegetable shortening,
½ cup freshly grated Swiss cheese	cut into ¼-inch bits
1 tablespoon caraway seeds	3 to 4 tablespoons ice water
¼ teaspoon table salt	1 egg, lightly beaten
6 tablespoons butter, chilled and cut	2 tablespoons coarse (kosher) salt

Place the flour, cheese, caraway seeds and table salt in a deep mixing bowl. Add the butter and shortening bits and, with your fingertips, rub the flour and fat together until the mixture resembles flakes of coarse meal. Pour in 3 tablespoons of ice water all at once and mix with your fingers or a fork until the dough can be gathered into a compact ball. If the dough seems crumbly, add up to 1 tablespoon more ice water by drops until all the particles adhere. Divide the dough into two balls, wrap the balls in wax paper, and refrigerate for at least 1 hour.

Preheat the oven to 375°. On a lightly floured surface, roll out one ball of the dough into a 12-inch square about ¼ inch thick. With a ruler and a pastry wheel or sharp knife, cut the square in half crosswise and then lengthwise into ½-inch-wide strips to make about 4 dozen 6-by-½-inch strips. With a pastry brush, spread about half of the beaten egg lightly but evenly over the top of the strips, and sprinkle the entire surface with 1 tablespoon of the coarse salt. Repeat the entire process with the second ball of dough. When you finish you should have a total of 8 dozen strips of prepared dough.

To shape each caraway twist, press two strips of dough together, salt sides out. Pinch the strips tightly at one end and, with your fingers, gently wind the two strips together lengthwise to form a long loose spiral.

With a large metal spatula, carefully arrange the caraway twists on two ungreased baking sheets and bake them in the middle of the oven for

8 to 10 minutes, or until they are crisp and golden brown. Slide the twists onto wire racks to cool to room temperature before serving them. In a tightly covered jar or tin, they can safely be kept for a week or two.

Zucchini Victor

To serve 4 to 6 as a first course

1 large firm ripe zucchini (about 1 pound)	¼ cup distilled white vinegar
1 large firm ripe yellow straightneck squash (about 1 pound)	¼ teaspoon salt
	⅛ teaspoon ground white pepper
5 cups chicken stock, fresh or canned	⅔ cup olive oil
	1 canned pimiento, drained and cut lengthwise into ⅛-inch-wide strips
2 celery tops, 8 fresh parsley sprigs and 1 medium-sized bay leaf, tied together with string	8 flat anchovy fillets, drained
	Sprigs of watercress for garnish

Zucchini Victor is adapted from celery Victor—a poached-celery salad created by chef Victor Hirtzler of the St. Francis Hotel in San Francisco.

Using a vegetable brush, scrub the zucchini and straightneck squash thoroughly under cold running water and pat them dry with paper towels. With a sharp knife, remove the stems and cut both squash in half crosswise. Then slice each half lengthwise into eight thin strips.

In a heavy 3- to 4-quart saucepan, bring the chicken stock and the tied celery leaves, parsley sprigs and bay leaf to a boil over high heat. Add the squash, cover the pan partially, and reduce the heat to moderate. Cook for about 5 minutes, or until a slice of squash shows only slight resistance when pierced with the point of a small sharp knife. Pick out and discard the tied herbs and drain the squash in a sieve or colander. (If you like, you may drain the stock into a bowl and reserve it for another use.)

Meanwhile, combine the vinegar, salt and pepper in a deep bowl and stir with a wire whisk until the salt dissolves. Whisking constantly, pour in the olive oil in a slow, thin stream and beat until the marinade mixture is thick and smooth. Taste for seasoning. Add the squash and turn the pieces about gently with a spoon to coat them evenly. Then cover the bowl tightly with foil or plastic wrap and marinate the squash in the refrigerator for about 12 hours or overnight.

To serve, transfer the squash to a chilled platter with a slotted spoon. Moisten the squash with a few spoonfuls of the marinade and arrange the pimiento strips and anchovies attractively on top. Garnish the platter with watercress and serve at once.

Cheese Balls

To make about 2 dozen 1-inch balls

1 cup freshly grated Monterey Jack cheese plus 1 cup freshly grated Cheddar or longhorn cheese, or 2 cups any combination of these cheeses
2 tablespoons flour
1 cup fresh cracker crumbs, made from saltines pulverized in a blender or wrapped in wax paper and finely crushed with a rolling pin
3 egg whites
1½ teaspoons prepared mustard
Vegetable oil for deep frying
Salt

Combine the grated cheese and flour in a deep mixing bowl and toss them together with a spoon. Spread the cracker crumbs on a piece of wax paper and set aside.

With a wire whisk or a rotary or electric beater, beat the egg whites until they are stiff enough to stand in unwavering peaks on the whisk or beater when it is lifted from the bowl. Scoop the egg whites over the cheese mixture with a rubber spatula, add the mustard, and fold the ingredients together gently but thoroughly.

To make each cheese ball, scoop up a heaping tablespoonful of the cheese mixture and mold it into a ball by placing a second tablespoon on top. Slide the cheese ball off the spoon onto the cracker crumbs and roll it about to coat it evenly. Transfer the cheese ball to a piece of wax paper and set it aside while you proceed to shape and coat the remaining balls. (At this stage, the cheese balls can be draped with wax paper and refrigerated for up to 12 hours or overnight if you like.)

Pour vegetable oil into a deep fryer or large heavy saucepan to a depth of about 3 inches and heat the oil until it reaches a temperature of 375° on a deep-frying thermometer.

Deep-fry the cheese balls, four or five at a time, turning them about with a slotted spoon for about 3 minutes, or until they are crisp and golden brown. As they color, transfer them to paper towels to drain.

Arrange the cheese balls attractively on a heated platter, season them lightly with a sprinkling of salt, and serve them while they are still warm as an accompaniment to drinks.

SOUPS

Sopa de Albóndigas
SPICED MEATBALL SOUP

To serve 6 to 8

2 tablespoons vegetable oil
½ cup finely chopped onions
1 teaspoon finely chopped garlic
2 quarts beef stock, fresh or canned
½ cup canned tomato purée
4 teaspoons finely chopped fresh hot green chilies *(caution: see note, page 3)*
1 teaspoon ground cumin
1 teaspoon ground coriander

1 pound ground lean beef
1 pound ground lean pork
½ cup raw long-grain white rice, not the converted variety
1 egg, lightly beaten
4 teaspoons finely cut fresh mint leaves
1½ teaspoons salt
½ teaspoon freshly ground black pepper

In a heavy 4- to 6-quart casserole, heat the oil over moderate heat until a light haze forms above it. Add the onions and garlic and, stirring frequently, cook for about 5 minutes, or until they are soft and translucent but not brown. Stir in the beef stock, tomato purée, chilies, cumin and coriander, and bring to a boil over high heat. Reduce the heat to low and simmer partially covered for 20 minutes.

Meanwhile, combine the beef, pork, rice, egg, mint leaves, salt and pepper in a deep bowl and knead the ingredients together vigorously with both hands. Then beat with a large wooden spoon until the mixture is light and fluffy. To shape each meatball, scoop up about 2 teaspoons of the mixture and roll it into a ball about ½ inch in diameter.

Drop the meatballs into the simmering stock mixture and stir gently to prevent them from sticking to one another. Cover the casserole partially and simmer the soup for about 30 minutes longer.

Taste for seasoning and ladle the *sopa de albóndigas* into a heated tureen or individual soup plates. Serve at once.

Artichoke Soup

To serve 6 to 8

Two 12- to 14-ounce artichokes
6 cups chicken stock, fresh or
    canned
¼ cup strained fresh lemon juice
1 cup cold water combined with
    1 tablespoon strained fresh lemon

    juice
2 tablespoons butter
2 tablespoons finely chopped
    shallots
2 tablespoons flour
1 cup light cream

With a small sharp knife, trim about ⅛ inch off the stem end of each artichoke and peel the tough outer skin from the remaining stem. Cut the artichokes lengthwise in half, drop them into a 4- to 5-quart enameled or stainless-steel saucepan, and pour in the chicken stock and the ¼ cup of lemon juice. Bring to a boil over high heat, reduce the heat to low, cover the pan partially and simmer the artichokes for 20 to 30 minutes, or until their bases show no resistance when pierced with the point of a small sharp knife.

With tongs or a slotted spoon, transfer the artichokes to a cutting board. Cut or pull off the green artichoke leaves, return them to the saucepan, and simmer partially covered for 10 minutes longer.

Meanwhile, cut or pull the thistlelike yellow leaves and hairy inner chokes away from the artichoke bottoms *(drawings, opposite)* and discard them. Trim the artichoke bottoms, drop them into a bowl and pour the water-and-lemon-juice mixture over them. Set the bottoms aside; they can safely wait at room temperature for 2 or 3 hours.

Scoop the green leaves out of the stock with a slotted spoon. With a teaspoon, scrape the soft flesh from each artichoke leaf. Return the pulp to the stock and discard the scraped leaves. Simmer the stock, partially covered, for 30 minutes more, then purée the mixture through a food mill set over a bowl or rub it through a fine sieve with the back of a spoon.

In a heavy 3- to 4-quart saucepan, melt the butter over moderate heat. When the foam begins to subside, add the shallots and stir for about 5 minutes, or until they are soft and translucent but not brown. Mix in the flour and stir over low heat for 2 or 3 minutes to remove the taste of raw flour. Stirring the mixture constantly, pour in the artichoke purée in a slow, thin stream and cook over high heat until the soup comes to a boil, thickens slightly and is smooth. Stir in the cream, simmer for 2 or 3 minutes, then taste for seasoning. Pour the soup into a bowl and cool it to room temperature. Cover with foil or plastic wrap and refrigerate for 1 or 2 hours, or until the soup is thoroughly chilled.

Just before serving, rinse the artichoke bottoms briefly under cold running water, pat them completely dry with paper towels and cut them into ¼-inch dice. Pour the soup into a chilled tureen or individual soup plates, scatter the pieces of artichoke bottom on top and serve at once.

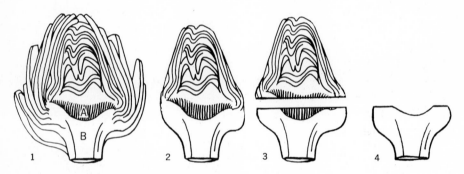

HOW TO PREPARE AN ARTICHOKE BOTTOM

Diced artichoke bottoms, like the ones scattered over the chilled artichoke soup *(opposite)*, are among the most elegant of all vegetable garnitures. Care must be taken, however, in freeing a whole artichoke bottom for dicing. (1) The bottom (B) is situated at the base of the artichoke, below the hairy choke (A), as shown in this cross section. (2) Cut or pull off the green outside leaves. (3) Cut off the yellow thistlelike leaves (part of the choke will be removed along with them) and discard them. (4) Pull or cut off the remainder of the choke. Then trim the edges of the bottom, cutting away as little as possible, and peel off the tough outer skin of the stem end. (When artichoke bottoms are served whole, the stem should be removed. But for a soup garniture, the stem may be diced with the artichoke bottom.) Immerse the artichoke bottom in lemon juice and water to prevent discoloration and let it stand at room temperature until you are ready to dice and serve it.

Bowl of the Wife of Kit Carson
TURKEY, CHICK-PEA AND GREEN CHILI SOUP

*When Sam Arnold built The Fort restaurant near Denver as a repro-
duction of a historic adobe fort, he sought out early foods as well. A
granddaughter of Kit Carson, the famed frontiersman, gave Mr. Arnold
the original family recipe for this savory turkey soup; he has embellished
it with a garnish of avocado slices.*

To serve 6 to 8

1 cup (½ pound) dried chick-peas
(*garbanzos*)

2 quarts water

Two 1½- to 2-pound turkey legs,
thoroughly defrosted if frozen

2 medium-sized onions, peeled and
coarsely chopped

1 medium-sized bay leaf, crumbled

1 tablespoon salt

8 whole black peppercorns

3 tablespoons uncooked long-grain
white rice (not the converted
variety)

1½ teaspoons crumbled dried
oregano

3 tablespoons finely chopped
seeded canned green chilies (not
the *jalapeño* variety; *caution: see
note, page 3*)

½ pound Monterey Jack cheese,
cut into ¼-inch dice, or
substitute ½ pound diced
Münster cheese

2 tablespoons finely chopped fresh
parsley

1 large firm ripe avocado, halved,
seeded, peeled and cut lengthwise
into thin slices (*see poor man's
butter, page 135*)

Starting a day ahead, wash the chick-peas in a sieve under cold running
water, place them in a large bowl or pan, and pour in enough cold water
to cover them by 2 inches. Soak at room temperature for at least 12 hours.

Drain the peas in a sieve or colander and discard the soaking water.
Then place the peas in a heavy 4- to 5-quart casserole, add the 2 quarts of
water, and bring to a boil over high heat. Reduce the heat to low and
simmer partially covered for about 1 hour, or until the chick-peas are
tender. With a slotted spoon, transfer them to a bowl and set aside.

Add the turkey legs to the chick-pea cooking liquid. The liquid should
cover the turkey completely; if necessary, add water. Bring to a boil over
high heat, meanwhile skimming off the foam and scum that rise to the
surface. Add the onions, bay leaf, salt and peppercorns, reduce the heat to
low, and simmer partially covered for about 45 minutes, or until the turkey
legs show no resistance when pierced deeply with the point of a small
sharp knife.

Transfer the turkey legs to a plate. Then strain the stock through a fine
sieve set over a bowl, and return it to the pot. Remove the skin from the
turkey legs with a small knife or your fingers. Cut or pull the meat away
from the bones and discard the skin and bones. Cut the meat into 1-inch
cubes and set them aside.

Over high heat, bring the stock in the casserole to a boil. Add the rice and oregano, stir well and reduce the heat to low. Cover tightly and simmer for 20 minutes, or until the rice is tender. Stir in the chick-peas, cubed turkey and chilies, and simmer for 4 or 5 minutes longer to heat all the ingredients through.

Taste for seasoning and ladle the soup into a heated tureen or serving bowl. Scatter the diced cheese and the parsley over the soup, arrange the avocado slices on top, and serve at once.

Mormon Split-Pea Soup

To serve 6 to 8

2 tablespoons butter	coarsely grated
1 cup finely chopped onions	½ teaspoon crumbled dried
½ cup finely chopped celery	marjoram
2 cups (1 pound) dried green split	3½ teaspoons salt
peas, washed in a sieve under	¼ teaspoon freshly ground black
cold running water	pepper
3 quarts water	1 pound lean ground pork
3 medium-sized boiling potatoes	1 teaspoon ground sage
(about 1 pound), peeled and	¼ teaspoon ground white pepper

In a heavy 5- to 6-quart casserole, melt the butter over moderate heat. When the foam begins to subside, add the onions and celery and, stirring frequently, cook for about 5 minutes, until the vegetables are soft but not brown. Stir in the peas and water, then bring to a boil over high heat, meanwhile skimming off the foam and scum that rise to the surface. Add the potatoes, marjoram, 2 teaspoons of the salt and the black pepper, reduce the heat to low, and simmer partially covered for 1 hour.

Meanwhile, combine the ground pork, sage, the remaining 1½ teaspoons of salt and the white pepper in a bowl. Knead vigorously with both hands, then beat with a wooden spoon until the mixture is smooth. Moistening your hands in cold water occasionally, pinch off about 1 tablespoon of the pork mixture at a time and shape each piece into a ball about 1 inch in diameter.

When the soup has cooked its allotted time, drop in the pork balls and return the soup to a simmer. Cover the pot partially and continue to simmer for 30 minutes. To test the pork for doneness, lift one of the balls out of the water with a slotted spoon and pierce it deeply with the point of a small sharp knife. If the liquid that trickles out is clear yellow, the pork is done even though the meat itself appears somewhat pink; however, if the liquid is pink, simmer the soup for 5 to 10 minutes longer.

Taste for seasoning and serve the soup at once.

Menudo
SPICY TRIPE-AND-PIG'S-FEET SOUP

To serve 8 to 12

3 pounds tripe, thoroughly
defrosted if frozen, cut into
1-inch squares
3 medium-sized onions, peeled and
quartered
8 whole black peppercorns
1 tablespoon plus 2 teaspoons salt
6 quarts cold water plus 1 quart
boiling water
3 pounds fresh pig's feet, sawed
(not chopped) into 3-inch pieces
6 dried *ancho* chilies
4 dried hot red chilies, each about
2 inches long *(caution: see note,
page 3)*
6 large garlic cloves, peeled
1 teaspoon dried oregano
A 1-pound 4-ounce can of hominy,
drained
1 tablespoon strained fresh lemon
juice

Place the tripe, two of the quartered onions, the peppercorns and 1 tablespoon of the salt in a heavy 7- to 8-quart casserole and pour in 4 quarts of the cold water. Bring to a boil over high heat, meanwhile skimming off the scum and foam as they rise to the surface. Reduce the heat to its lowest setting, cover the casserole partially and simmer for 3½ hours, or until the tripe is tender.

At the same time, combine the pig's feet, the remaining quartered onion, the remaining 2 teaspoons of salt and 2 quarts of cold water in another large heavy pot. Bring to a boil over high heat, skimming off the surface scum and foam, then reduce the heat to its lowest setting and simmer partially covered for 3½ hours, or until the pig's feet are tender.

While the tripe and pig's feet are simmering, prepare the chilies in the following manner: Under cold running water, pull the stems off the *ancho* and red chilies. Tear the chilies in half and brush out their seeds. Crumble the chilies coarsely, drop them into a bowl, and pour the 1 quart of boiling water over them. Let the chilies soak for at least 30 minutes, then drain them through a fine sieve set over a bowl and reserve the soaking water as well as the chilies.

Drain the tripe and pig's feet in a fine sieve or colander set over a deep bowl. Pick out and discard the onion quarters and peppercorns, then measure and reserve 9 cups of the combined cooking liquid. If there is less than 9 cups, add enough of the chili soaking liquid to make that amount.

Return the tripe to its casserole and transfer the pig's feet to a plate. With a small sharp knife cut the pig's feet meat away from the bones. Remove and discard the fat, gristle and skin and cut the meat into small pieces. Add the pieces of pig's feet meat to the tripe.

Combine the chilies, garlic, oregano and 1 cup of the reserved cooking liquid in the jar of an electric blender and blend at high speed for 30 seconds. Turn off the machine, scrape down the sides of the jar with a rubber spatula and blend again until the chili mixture is a smooth purée.

Add the chili purée and the remaining 8 cups of reserved cooking liquid to the meats. Stir in the hominy and bring to a simmer over moderate heat. Reduce the heat to its lowest setting and simmer gently, partially covered, for 30 minutes.

Stir in the lemon juice and taste for seasoning. Ladle the *menudo* into a heated tureen or individual soup plates and serve at once. Or, if you prefer, cool it to room temperature, cover tightly and refrigerate. Then reheat it briefly before serving. *Menudo* is traditionally served as a midnight supper or in the morning following a late party.

Dill Soup

To serve 8

6 tablespoons butter
1 cup finely chopped onions
1 cup coarsely chopped celery
2 medium-sized carrots, scraped and sliced into ⅛-inch-thick rounds
2 one-pound cans tomatoes, drained and chopped, with all liquid reserved
2 large boiling potatoes, peeled and cut into ½-inch cubes
1 small fresh cauliflower, trimmed and separated into flowerets

2 quarts chicken stock, fresh or canned
2 teaspoons salt
Freshly ground black pepper
A large bunch of fresh dill leaves, tied together with string
½ pound fresh green string beans, trimmed and cut into 2-inch lengths
1 pound fresh green peas, shelled, or one 10-ounce package frozen peas, thoroughly defrosted
Fresh dill sprigs for garnish

In a heavy 5- to 6-quart pot, melt the butter over moderate heat. When the foam begins to subside, add the onions, celery and carrots, and stir frequently for about 5 minutes, or until the vegetables are soft but not brown. Stir in the tomatoes and their liquid, the potatoes, cauliflower, stock, salt and a liberal grinding of pepper. Bring to a boil over high heat, reduce the heat to low and simmer partially covered for 30 minutes.

Add the dill, string beans and peas, and simmer partially covered for 15 minutes longer, or until all the vegetables are tender but still intact. Pick out and discard the dill and taste the soup for seasoning. Ladle the soup into a heated tureen or individual heated soup plates, garnish with sprigs of fresh dill, and serve at once.

SALADS & DRESSINGS

Caviar-Potato Salad

To serve 6

6 medium-sized boiling potatoes
  (about 2 pounds)
¼ cup cider vinegar
½ cup finely chopped onions
A 2-ounce jar of red caviar
1 cup freshly made mayonnaise
  (page 29), or substitute 1 cup

  unsweetened bottled mayonnaise
½ cup sour cream
2 tablespoons finely cut fresh dill
1 teaspoon salt
½ teaspoon freshly ground black
  pepper
Sprigs of dill for garnish (optional)

Drop the potatoes into enough boiling water to cover them completely. Cook briskly, uncovered, until the potatoes are tender and show no resistance when pierced deeply with the point of a small sharp knife. Drain the potatoes in a sieve or colander and, while they are still warm, peel and cut them into ½-inch-thick slices. Place the slices in a bowl, add the vinegar and onions, and toss together gently but thoroughly with a spoon.

Drain the caviar in a small strainer and run cold water over the grains to remove the excess salt. Spread the grains on paper towels and gently pat them dry with fresh paper towels. Reserve about 1 teaspoon of caviar to garnish the salad and place the rest in a bowl. With a rubber spatula, stir in the mayonnaise, sour cream, dill, salt and pepper, and taste for seasoning. Pour the mixture over the potatoes and with the spatula toss gently until the slices are evenly coated.

Mound the salad in a serving bowl, spread the reserved teaspoon of caviar on top and garnish it with sprigs of dill if desired. Serve at once.

Ginger-Ale Salad

To serve 6 to 8

1 tablespoon vegetable oil
1 small Temple or navel orange
½ cup cold water
1 envelope unflavored gelatin
¼ cup sugar
1½ cups ginger ale
2 tablespoons strained fresh lemon
    juice
2 medium-sized firm ripe peaches,
    peeled, halved, pitted and cut

lengthwise into ⅓-inch-thick
    slices
½ cup fresh ripe strawberries,
    washed, hulled and cut
    lengthwise into ⅓-inch-thick
    slices
½ cup table grapes, washed,
    halved and seeded if necessary
1 tablespoon very finely chopped
    crystallized ginger

With a pastry brush, spread the vegetable oil evenly inside a 1-quart decorative mold. Invert the mold on paper towels to drain off the excess oil.

Remove the peel and all of the white membrane of the orange with a small sharp knife, using short sawing motions. Section the orange by cutting along both sides of each membrane division to the core. As each section is freed, carefully lift it out and set it aside on paper towels to drain.

Pour the water into a heatproof measuring cup and sprinkle the gelatin over it. When the gelatin has softened for 2 or 3 minutes, set the cup in a small skillet of simmering water and stir over low heat until the gelatin dissolves completely. Add the sugar and stir until it dissolves.

Pour the gelatin mixture into a deep bowl and stir in the ginger ale and lemon juice. Then set the bowl into a larger bowl half filled with crushed ice or ice cubes and cold water. With a metal spoon, stir the mixture until it thickens enough to flow sluggishly off the spoon. Stir in the orange sections, peaches, strawberries, grapes and the crystallized ginger.

Pour the mixture into the oiled mold, cover with foil or plastic wrap, and refrigerate for at least 4 hours, or until it is firm to the touch.

To unmold the salad, run a thin knife around the sides of the mold and dip the bottom briefly into hot water. Place an inverted serving plate on top of the mold and, grasping plate and mold together firmly, turn them over. Rap the plate on a table and the ginger-ale salad should slide out easily. Refrigerate until ready to serve. Ginger-ale salad may be served with poppy-seed or strawberry-and-sour-cream dressing *(page 27)*.

Beer Coleslaw

To serve 4 to 6

A 2- to 3-pound green cabbage
3 tablespoons finely chopped onion
½ green bell pepper, washed,
  seeded, deribbed and cut into
  strips ¼ inch wide and 1 inch
  long

1 cup freshly made mayonnaise
  (page 29), or substitute 1 cup
  unsweetened bottled mayonnaise
¼ cup beer
1 teaspoon celery seed
½ teaspoon salt
Freshly ground black pepper

Wash the cabbage under cold running water, remove the tough outer leaves, and cut the cabbage into quarters. To shred the cabbage, cut out the core and slice the quarters crosswise into ⅛-inch-wide strips. Drop the cabbage into a large mixing bowl, add the onion and bell pepper, and mix well with a spoon.

In a small bowl, combine the mayonnaise, beer, celery seed, salt and a few grindings of black pepper and stir with a wire whisk until all the ingredients are blended. Then pour the mixture over the cabbage and toss together gently but thoroughly. Taste for seasoning.

Cover the bowl with plastic wrap and refrigerate the coleslaw for about an hour before serving.

Molded Horseradish Salad

To serve 6 to 8 as an
  accompaniment to meats

1 tablespoon vegetable oil
2 cups beef stock, fresh or canned
1 envelope unflavored gelatin
¼ cup sugar
1 teaspoon salt

2 tablespoons strained fresh lemon
  juice
A 4-ounce bottle of prepared
  horseradish, drained in a sieve
  and squeezed completely dry

With a pastry brush, brush the inside surfaces of a 2-cup mold evenly with the vegetable oil. Then invert the mold on paper towels to drain.

Pour ½ cup of the beef stock into a small saucepan, add the gelatin and let it soften for 2 or 3 minutes. Place the pan over low heat and, stirring constantly, cook until the gelatin dissolves. Add the remaining 1½ cups of beef stock, the sugar, salt and lemon juice, and continue to stir over low heat until the sugar dissolves.

Pour the gelatin mixture into a bowl and set it inside a larger bowl half filled with crushed ice or ice cubes and water. Stir with a metal spoon until the gelatin is cold and thick, then add the horseradish and mix well. Pour the gelatin-horseradish mixture into the prepared mold, cover with foil or plastic wrap and refrigerate the salad for at least 2 hours, or until it is firm to the touch.

To unmold and serve the horseradish salad, run the blade of a knife around the inside edge of the mold to loosen the sides. Dip the bottom of the mold briefly in hot water. Place an inverted serving plate over the mold and, grasping plate and mold together firmly, turn them over. The molded horseradish salad should slide out easily. Serve at once as an accompaniment to cold meats.

Spinach-and-Bacon Salad

To serve 4

1 pound fresh young spinach	juice
4 slices lean bacon	½ teaspoon sugar
¼ cup olive oil	1 teaspoon salt
¼ cup red wine vinegar	¼ teaspoon freshly ground black
2 tablespoons strained fresh lemon	pepper

Wash the spinach thoroughly in a colander set under cold running water and tear off and discard the tough stems and any blemished leaves. Spread the spinach on paper towels to drain and pat the leaves completely dry with fresh paper towels. Then tear the leaves into 1-inch pieces, drop them into a salad bowl and set aside.

Prepare the dressing in the following manner: In a heavy 8- to 10-inch skillet, fry the bacon over moderate heat, turning the slices frequently with tongs until they are crisp and brown. Transfer the bacon slices to paper towels to drain, then crumble them into bits.

Pour off the fat remaining in the skillet and in its place add the olive oil. Return the bacon bits to the skillet and stir over high heat for a few seconds. Remove the skillet from the heat and stir in the vinegar, lemon juice, sugar, salt and pepper. Taste the dressing for seasoning, pour it over the spinach and toss the leaves about with a spoon to coat them evenly. Serve at once.

Lime-Gelatin Salad

To serve 6 to 8

1 medium-sized firm ripe cucumber
1 teaspoon salt
1 tablespoon vegetable oil
2 packages lime-flavored gelatin
1 quart boiling water
2 eight-ounce packages cream
cheese, cut into ½-inch bits and
softened
2 tablespoons strained fresh lime
juice
2 teaspoons Worcestershire sauce
¼ teaspoon Tabasco sauce
1 cup finely chopped celery
¼ cup finely chopped onions
¼ cup finely cut fresh dill

With a small sharp knife, peel the cucumber and slice it lengthwise in half. Scoop out the seeds by running the tip of a teaspoon down the center of each half. Then cut the cucumber into ¼-inch dice. Place the dice in a fine sieve set over a bowl, add the salt and toss the cucumber about with a spoon to coat the dice evenly. Set aside to drain for at least 30 minutes, then pat the cucumber dice dry with paper towels.

Meanwhile, with a pastry brush, spread the vegetable oil evenly inside a 1-quart ring mold or eight individual 4-ounce molds. Invert the mold or molds on paper towels to allow the excess oil to drain off.

Place the powdered gelatin in a heatproof bowl, pour in the boiling water and mix well. Put the cream cheese in a large bowl, and with an electric mixer, beat it until it is light and fluffy. Beating the mixture constantly, pour in the gelatin in a slow thin stream and, when it is thoroughly incorporated, add the lime juice, Worcestershire sauce and Tabasco.

Set the bowl in a larger bowl half filled with crushed ice or ice cubes and cold water. Stir with a metal spoon until the gelatin mixture thickens enough to flow sluggishly off the spoon. Stir in the cucumber dice, the celery, onions and dill.

Pour the gelatin mixture into the oiled mold or molds, cover with plastic wrap and refrigerate for 4 hours, or until it is firm to the touch.

To unmold the salad, run a thin knife around the sides of the mold and dip the bottom briefly into hot water. Place an inverted serving plate on top of the mold and, grasping plate and mold together firmly, turn them over. Rap the plate on a table and the gelatin salad should slide out easily. Refrigerate until ready to serve.

Strawberry-and-Sour-Cream Dressing

To make about 2 cups

A 10-ounce package frozen sliced sweetened strawberries, thoroughly defrosted, and their syrup	1½ cups sour cream A pinch of salt Confectioners' sugar (optional)

Place the strawberries and their syrup in a bowl and crush the berries slightly with the back of a large spoon. Add the sour cream and salt, and stir until the ingredients are thoroughly blended. Taste for sweetness and add up to 1 tablespoon of confectioners' sugar if desired. Cover with foil or plastic wrap and refrigerate the dressing for at least 1 hour before serving. Strawberry-and-sour-cream dressing may accompany any fruit salad.

Poppy-Seed Dressing

To make about 2½ cups

	2 teaspoons dry mustard
⅔ cup white distilled vinegar	2 teaspoons salt
2 teaspoons finely grated onion	2 cups vegetable oil
1 cup sugar	3 tablespoons poppy seeds

Combine the vinegar, onion, sugar, mustard and salt in a bowl and stir vigorously with a wire whisk until the sugar, mustard and salt dissolve. Whisking constantly, pour in the oil in a slow, thin stream and continue to beat until the dressing is smooth and thick. Stir in the poppy seeds and taste for seasoning.

Serve the poppy-seed dressing at once with any fruit salad or cover tightly with plastic wrap and store in a cool place or the refrigerator until ready to serve. Tightly covered and refrigerated, the dressing can safely be kept for 6 to 10 days.

Yoghurt-and-Honey Dressing

To make about 1 cup

1 cup (8 ounces) plain unflavored
   yoghurt
2 tablespoons honey

1 tablespoon finely cut fresh mint
   leaves
1 to 2 teaspoons strained fresh
   lemon juice

Combine the yoghurt, honey and mint in a bowl and beat with a wire whisk until the mixture is smooth. Whisk in 1 teaspoon of the lemon juice, then taste the dressing and add up to 1 teaspoon more lemon juice if desired. Cover tightly with foil or plastic wrap and refrigerate until ready to serve.

Yoghurt-and-honey dressing may be served with any fruit salad.

Apricot-Cream Dressing

To make about 3 cups

½ cup dried apricots
3 tablespoons confectioners' sugar
1 cup heavy cream, chilled

Place the apricots in a bowl and pour in enough boiling water to cover them completely. Let them soak for 10 to 15 minutes, or until they are soft, then drain them in a sieve set over a bowl. Combine the apricots and ¼ cup of the soaking liquid in the jar of an electric blender and blend at medium speed for 15 seconds. Turn the machine off, scrape down the sides of the jar with a rubber spatula and blend again until the apricots are a smooth purée. Scrape the purée into a bowl and stir in the sugar.

In a chilled bowl, whip the cream with a wire whisk or a rotary or electric beater until stiff enough to stand in unwavering peaks on the beater when it is lifted from the bowl. With a rubber spatula, scoop the apricot purée over the cream and fold them together gently but thoroughly.

Taste the apricot-cream dressing for sweetness and serve it with any fruit salad. Tightly covered with plastic wrap, the dressing can safely be stored in the refrigerator for up to 3 hours before serving.

Mayonnaise
To make about 2 cups

3 egg yolks, at room temperature
1 to 3 teaspoons strained fresh
   lemon juice
½ teaspoon dry mustard
½ teaspoon salt
⅛ teaspoon ground white pepper
1½ cups vegetable or olive oil or
   a combination of both
2 tablespoons boiling water
   (optional)

Warm a small mixing bowl in hot water, dry it quickly but thoroughly, and drop in the egg yolks. With a wire whisk or a rotary or electric beater, beat the yolks vigorously for about 2 minutes, until they thicken and cling to the whisk or beater when it is lifted from the bowl. Stir in 1 teaspoon of lemon juice and the mustard, salt and white pepper.

Beat in ½ cup of the oil ½ teaspoon at a time; make sure each addition is absorbed before adding more. By the time the ½ cup of oil has been beaten in, the sauce should be the consistency of thick cream. Pour in the remaining oil in a slow, thin stream, beating constantly. Then taste for seasoning and add up to 2 more teaspoons of lemon juice if desired.

To make the mayonnaise creamier and lessen the danger of separating, beat in the boiling water, 1 tablespoon at a time. Cover the mayonnaise tightly with foil or plastic wrap and refrigerate until ready to use. The mayonnaise can safely be kept in the refrigerator for up to one week.

VEGETABLES & GARNISHES

Basque Sheepherders' Potatoes

To serve 6 to 8

3 tablespoons bacon fat
9 medium-sized boiling potatoes
  (about 3 pounds), peeled and cut
  crosswise into ⅛-inch-thick
  slices
Salt

Freshly ground black pepper
4 eggs
2 tablespoons finely cut fresh chives
1 tablespoon finely chopped fresh
  parsley
¼ teaspoon crumbled dried thyme

Preheat the oven to 375°. Put 2 tablespoons of the bacon fat into a 10-inch enameled or cast-iron skillet and tip the pan from side to side to spread the fat evenly. Arrange about one third of the potato slices in a flat layer in the skillet and season them lightly with salt and pepper. Repeat two more times, then dribble or dot the remaining tablespoon of bacon fat over the top. Cover tightly and bake in the middle of the oven for about 1 hour, or until the potatoes are tender.

Beat the eggs lightly with a wire whisk or a fork, add the chives, parsley and thyme, and mix well. Then pour the egg mixture over the potatoes, cover again and continue baking for 5 minutes, or until the eggs are just firm to the touch. Do not overcook.

To unmold and serve the sheepherders' potatoes, loosen the edges by running a knife around the sides of the skillet and as far beneath the potatoes as possible without breaking them apart. Place an inverted plate on top of the skillet and, grasping plate and skillet together firmly, turn them over. The potatoes should slide out easily. Serve at once.

Stuffed Baked Potatoes with Sour Cream
To serve 8

3 tablespoons butter, softened, plus
  6 tablespoons butter, melted and
  cooled
10 six-ounce baking potatoes,
  thoroughly scrubbed and patted
dry with paper towels
1 teaspoon salt
¼ teaspoon ground white pepper
½ cup sour cream
2 egg yolks

Preheat the oven to 350°. With a pastry brush, spread 2 tablespoons of the softened butter over the skins of the potatoes. Bake the potatoes on a rack in the middle of the oven for about 45 minutes, until they feel soft when squeezed gently between your thumb and forefinger.

Cut a ¼-inch-thick slice lengthwise off the top of each baked potato. With a spoon, scoop the potato pulp into a bowl, leaving a boatlike shell about ¼ inch thick. Reserve the eight most uniform potato shells and discard the other two shells but retain their pulp.

Mash the potato pulp to a smooth purée with the back of a fork, or force the pulp through a ricer into a deep bowl. Add 4 tablespoons of the melted butter and the salt and pepper. In a small bowl, mix the sour cream and egg yolks together and beat the mixture into the potato purée. Taste for seasoning. Spoon the potato mixture into a pastry bag fitted with a No. 5B decorative tip, filling the bag no more than one third full, and pipe the mixture into the shells. Or spoon the mixture into the potato shells, mounding it slightly in the center. Brush a jelly-roll pan with the remaining tablespoon of softened butter and arrange the shells side by side in the pan.

If you wish to serve the potatoes at once, preheat the broiler to its highest setting. Brush the potatoes with the remaining 2 tablespoons of melted butter and slide them under the broiler for a minute or so to brown them.

If you prefer, the stuffed potatoes may be kept at room temperature for 2 or 3 hours before serving. In that event, preheat the oven to 400°, brush the potatoes with 2 tablespoons of melted butter and bake them in the middle of the oven for 15 or 20 minutes, or until they are golden brown and crusty.

Stuffed Baked Potatoes with Cheese
To serve 6

3 tablespoons butter, softened, plus
    4 tablespoons butter, cut into
    ¼-inch bits and softened
6 eight-ounce baking potatoes, each
    about 4 inches long, thoroughly
    scrubbed and patted dry with

paper towels
3¾ cups (about 1 pound) freshly
    grated sharp Cheddar cheese
½ cup sour cream
1 teaspoon salt
½ teaspoon ground white pepper

Preheat the oven to 350°. With a pastry brush, spread 2 tablespoons of the softened butter evenly over the skins of the potatoes. Bake the potatoes on a rack set in the middle of the oven for about 45 minutes. The potatoes are fully baked if they feel soft when squeezed gently between your thumb and forefinger.

Cut a ¼-inch-thick lengthwise slice from each baked potato. With a spoon, scoop the potato pulp into a bowl, leaving a boatlike shell about ¼ inch thick. Set the potato shells aside.

Mash the pulp to a smooth purée with the back of a fork, or force the pulp through a ricer or food mill into a deep bowl. Add 3 cups of the grated cheese and mix well. Then beat in the sour cream and, when it is completely incorporated, add the 4 tablespoons of butter bits, the salt and the pepper. Taste for seasoning.

Spoon the potato mixture into a large pastry bag fitted with a No. 5B decorative tip and pipe it into the reserved potato shells. Or spoon the mixture directly into the potato shells, dividing it equally among them and mounding it slightly in the center of each one. Brush a jelly-roll pan evenly with the remaining tablespoon of softened butter and arrange the stuffed potato shells side by side in the pan.

If you wish to serve the potatoes at once, preheat the broiler to its highest setting. Sprinkle the remaining ¾ cup of grated cheese evenly over the potatoes, then slide them under the broiler for a minute or two to melt the topping.

If you prefer, the stuffed potatoes may be arranged on the buttered pan, draped with wax paper and kept at room temperature for 2 or 3 hours before serving.

In that event, preheat the oven to 400°, sprinkle the ¾ cup of grated cheese over the potatoes, and bake the potatoes in the middle of the oven for 15 to 20 minutes, or until they are heated through and the tops are golden brown and crusty. Serve them at once.

Hashed Brown Potatoes

To serve 4

½ pound butter, cut into ¼-inch
  bits
5 medium-sized boiling potatoes
  (about 1½ pounds)
1 teaspoon salt
Freshly ground black pepper

First clarify the butter in the following fashion: In a small heavy sauce-pan, melt the butter bits over low heat, stirring so that they melt com-pletely without browning. Remove from the heat and let the butter rest for a minute or so, then skim off the foam and discard it. Tipping the pan slightly, spoon the clear butter into a bowl and discard the milky sol-ids on the bottom of the pan. Set the clarified butter aside.

Peel the potatoes and, as you proceed, drop them into cold water to pre-vent their discoloring. One at a time, pat the potatoes dry with paper tow-els and grate them onto wax paper through the teardrop-shaped holes on a stand-up hand grater. Wrap the grated potatoes in a kitchen towel and squeeze gently to remove their excess moisture.

Ladle ⅓ cup of the clarified butter into a heavy 12-inch skillet, pref-erably one with a nonstick surface. Warm the butter over moderate heat, then place the grated potatoes in the center of the pan and season them with the salt and pepper. Using a large metal spatula, mash and shape the potatoes into four oblong or round cakes each about ½ inch thick.

Fry the potatoes over high heat for about 2 minutes, sliding the pan back and forth occasionally to prevent the underside of the cakes from sticking. Then reduce the heat to moderate and fry for 2 or 3 minutes long-er, or until the undersides of the cakes are golden brown.

Carefully turn the potatoes over with the spatula and pour the re-maining clarified butter around them. Fry the cakes over high heat for about 2 minutes, sliding the pan back and forth occasionally. Reduce the heat to moderate and fry for about 3 minutes more, or until the other sides of the cakes are golden brown.

Tip the pan slightly and slide the hashed brown potatoes onto a heated platter. Serve at once.

Cebollas Rellenas
BAKED ONIONS WITH MEAT-AND-CHILI STUFFING

To serve 4

1 tablespoon butter, softened, plus
   1 tablespoon butter, cut into
   ¼-inch bits
4 eight-ounce onions, unpeeled
½ cup finely chopped leftover
   cooked beef, lamb or pork
8 tablespoons (½ cup) soft fresh
   crumbs made from homemade-
   type bread pulverized in a

blender or finely shredded with a
   fork
½ cup finely chopped seeded
   drained canned red chilies
1 tablespoon finely chopped fresh
   parsley
½ teaspoon crumbled dried
   oregano
½ teaspoon salt

Preheat the oven to 375°. With a pastry brush, spread the tablespoon of softened butter evenly over the bottom and sides of a shallow baking dish large enough to hold the onions in one layer. Set it aside.

In a heavy 3- to 4-quart saucepan, bring 2 quarts of water to a boil over high heat. Drop in the unpeeled onions and boil them briskly, uncovered, for 10 minutes. Drain the onions in a sieve or colander and, when they are cool enough to handle, cut off the root ends with a small sharp knife and slip off the papery outer skins. Cut a slice about 1 inch thick off the top of each onion and discard the slice. With a fork pull out the centers of the onions to make cuplike shells about ¼ inch thick, composed of the two or three outermost layers of the onion. Invert the onion shells on paper towels to drain, and finely chop enough of the scooped-out onion centers to make ¼ cup.

Combine the meat, 6 tablespoons of the bread crumbs, the chopped onions, chilies, parsley, oregano and salt in a bowl, and stir until the ingredients are thoroughly blended. Taste for seasoning. Spoon the meat mixture into the onion shells, dividing it equally among them.

Arrange the stuffed onions side by side in the buttered baking dish, sprinkle them with the remaining 2 tablespoons of bread crumbs and dot the tops with the tablespoon of butter bits. Carefully pour ½ cup of boiling water into the bottom of the dish and bake the onions in the middle of the oven for 20 to 30 minutes, or until the tops are brown and the onions are tender but not falling apart. With a spatula, transfer the onions to a heated platter and serve at once.

NOTE: If you do not have cooked meat at hand, fry ¼ pound of ground beef in 2 tablespoons of butter until no trace of pink remains. Drain the beef in a sieve to remove the excess fat before stuffing the onions.

Calabacitas Agrias y Dulces
SWEET-AND-SOUR SQUASH

To serve 4

¼ pound dried apples
4 tablespoons butter
1 pound firm young zucchini or
  yellow straightneck squash,
  thoroughly scrubbed but not
  peeled, and cut into ½-inch
  chunks
½ teaspoon crumbled dried basil
½ teaspoon salt
¼ cup cider vinegar
2 tablespoons light brown sugar

If the dried apples are moist and flexible, place them in a bowl, pour in enough boiling water to cover them and let the apples soak for about 30 minutes. If the dried apples are stiff and brittle, cover them with cold water, set the bowl in the refrigerator and let the apples soak overnight. In either case, drain the apples in a sieve, discarding the water, and pat them completely dry with paper towels.

Preheat the oven to 350°. In a heavy 10- to 12-inch skillet, melt the butter over moderate heat. When the foam begins to subside, add the apples and squash and, stirring frequently, cook for about 5 minutes, until they are delicately browned. Stir in the basil and salt and then, with a slotted spoon, transfer the apples and squash to a deep 1-quart baking dish.

Add the vinegar and sugar to the butter remaining in the skillet and stir over high heat for 3 or 4 minutes. When the mixture thickens slightly, pour it into the baking dish and toss the pieces of squash and apple about with a spoon until they are lightly and evenly coated. Bake in the middle of the oven for 20 to 25 minutes, or until the squash is tender and shows no resistance when pierced with the point of a small sharp knife. Serve at once, directly from the baking dish.

Eggplant-Banana Casserole
To serve 4

1 medium-sized eggplant (about 1 pound), cut lengthwise into ¼-inch-thick slices
2 teaspoons salt
1 teaspoon crumbled dried thyme
½ teaspoon freshly ground black pepper
½ to 1 cup vegetable oil

1 tablespoon butter, softened, plus 4 tablespoons butter, cut into ½-inch bits
3 large ripe bananas, peeled and cut lengthwise into halves
¾ teaspoon ground nutmeg, preferably freshly grated
3 large firm ripe tomatoes

Sprinkle the eggplant slices lightly with 1 teaspoon of the salt, lay them side by side between two layers of paper towels and weight them down with a large heavy platter or casserole. Let them rest for 20 to 30 minutes, then pat them dry with fresh paper towels. Season the eggplant slices on both sides with the thyme and black pepper.

In a heavy 12-inch skillet, bring ½ cup of the vegetable oil almost to the smoking point over high heat. Add a few slices of the eggplant and cook them for a minute or two on each side, regulating the heat so that they color quickly without burning. Transfer them to paper towels to drain and brown the remaining eggplant, a few slices at a time, adding up to ½ cup more oil to the skillet as necessary.

Meanwhile, preheat the oven to 350°. With a pastry brush, spread the tablespoon of softened butter evenly over the bottom and sides of a 1½-quart baking dish at least 2 inches deep, and set it aside.

Melt the 4 tablespoons of butter bits over moderate heat in a heavy 12-inch skillet. When the foam begins to subside, add the banana halves and, turning them once with tongs, fry for about 2 minutes on each side, or until they are golden brown. Remove the pan from the heat and sprinkle the bananas with the nutmeg.

Drop the tomatoes into enough boiling water to cover them completely. After 15 seconds remove the tomatoes and run them under cold water. With a small sharp knife, remove the stems, peel the tomatoes and slice them into ¼-inch-thick rounds. Season the tomatoes with the remaining teaspoon of salt.

Before assembling the casserole, spread the eggplant slices on paper towels and set aside the two most attractive slices. Arrange about half of the remaining slices in the bottom of the buttered dish, set three banana halves side by side over them and cover with half of the tomato slices. Repeat the layers with the rest of the eggplant, bananas and tomatoes, and place the two reserved eggplant slices on top.

Bake in the middle of the oven for 30 minutes, or until the top has begun to bubble. Serve at once, directly from the baking dish.

Colache

VEGETABLE STEW

To serve 4 to 6

2 tablespoons vegetable oil
1 cup finely chopped onions
1 teaspoon finely chopped garlic
2 pounds firm young zucchini or
  yellow straightneck squash,
  thoroughly scrubbed but not
  peeled, and cut crosswise into
  ¼-inch-thick slices
1 pound fresh green string beans,
  trimmed, washed and cut
  crosswise into 1½-inch lengths
1 teaspoon finely chopped fresh hot
  green chilies *(caution: see note,
  page 3)*
4 medium-sized firm ripe tomatoes,
  peeled, seeded and coarsely
  chopped *(see chili con queso,
  page 8)*, or substitute 1½
  cups chopped drained canned
  tomatoes
2 teaspoons salt
¼ teaspoon freshly ground black
  pepper
1 cup fresh corn kernels, cut from
  about 2 large ears of corn

In a heavy 7- to 8-quart casserole, heat the oil over moderate heat until a light haze forms above it. Add the onions and garlic and, stirring frequently, cook for about 5 minutes, or until they are soft and translucent but not brown. Add the zucchini, string beans and chilies, and stir for 2 or 3 minutes. Then stir in the tomatoes, salt and pepper. Reduce the heat to low, cover the casserole partially and simmer for 15 minutes. Add the corn, mix well and continue to simmer partially covered until the zucchini and string beans are tender but still somewhat crisp to the bite. Taste for seasoning and serve at once, directly from the casserole.

NOTE: If you like, you may cut the ears of corn crosswise into 2-inch chunks rather than removing the kernels. Drop the corn chunks into enough lightly salted boiling water to cover them by at least 1 inch. At once, cover the pot and remove it from the heat. Let the corn stand for 5 minutes, then drain it in a colander or sieve. Add the chunks to the *colache* as described above and simmer them with the other vegetables for about 5 minutes before serving.

Deep-fried Okra

To serve 4

1 pound fresh okra, or substitute
    two 10-ounce packages frozen
    okra, thoroughly defrosted

Salt
Vegetable oil for deep frying
2 eggs
1 cup yellow cornmeal

Wash the fresh okra under cold running water, and with a small sharp knife scrape the skin lightly to remove any surface fuzz. (Frozen okra needs only to be defrosted and drained.) Pat the okra dry with paper towels, cut off the stems and slice the okra crosswise into 1-inch-long rounds. Combine the okra and 1 teaspoon of salt in a bowl and turn the pieces about with a spoon to season them evenly.

Pour vegetable oil into a deep fryer or large heavy saucepan to a depth of about 3 inches and heat the oil until it reaches a temperature of 335° on a deep-frying thermometer.

Break the eggs into a shallow bowl and beat them to a froth with a wire whisk or a table fork. Spread the cornmeal out on a sheet of wax paper. Immerse two or three rounds of okra in the eggs, roll them in the cornmeal to coat both sides and drop them into the hot oil. Deep-fry for 5 to 6 minutes, or until they are crisp and golden brown. As they brown, transfer them to paper towels to drain while you deep-fry the remaining okra.

Sprinkle the deep-fried okra lightly with salt, arrange the pieces attractively on a heated platter and serve at once.

Okra and Tomatoes

To serve 4

1 pound fresh okra, or substitute
    two 10-ounce packages frozen
    okra, thoroughly defrosted
4 lean slices bacon, cut crosswise
    into halves
1 medium-sized onion, peeled and

    coarsely chopped
1½ teaspoons salt
3 medium-sized firm ripe tomatoes,
    peeled and coarsely chopped (see
    chile con queso, page 8)
1 teaspoon finely chopped fresh hot
    red chili (caution: see note, page 3)

Wash the fresh okra under cold running water, and with a small sharp knife scrape the skin lightly to remove any surface fuzz. (Frozen okra needs only to be thoroughly defrosted and drained.) Pat the okra completely dry with paper towels, cut off the stems and slice the okra crosswise into ¼-inch-thick rounds.

In a heavy 10-inch skillet, fry the bacon over moderate heat, turning the pieces frequently with tongs until they are crisp and brown and have rendered all their fat. Transfer the bacon to paper towels to drain.

Add the okra, onion and salt to the fat remaining in the skillet and, stirring constantly, cook over moderate heat for 10 minutes. Watch carefully and regulate the heat so that the vegetables do not burn. Add the tomatoes and chili and cook over high heat for 2 minutes, still stirring constantly. Reduce the heat to low and, stirring the mixture occasionally, simmer uncovered for about 15 minutes, or until the okra and tomatoes are soft. Taste for seasoning.

To serve, transfer the entire contents of the skillet to a heated bowl and arrange the bacon on top.

Coliflor Fria
COLD SPICED CAULIFLOWER SALAD

To serve 4 to 6

1½ teaspoons whole black peppercorns	and cut into strips about 2 inches long and ⅛ inch wide *(caution: see note, page 3)*
¼ cup plus 1 tablespoon pine nuts *(pignolia)*	1 teaspoon salt
2 large garlic cloves, peeled and coarsely chopped	¼ cup distilled white vinegar
1 to 2 teaspoons finely chopped fresh hot red chilies plus 1 fresh hot red chili, stemmed, seeded	½ cup olive oil
	A 1-pound head of cauliflower, stemmed, trimmed and separated into small flowerets

Using a large mortar and pestle, crack the peppercorns into small bits. Add ¼ cup of the pine nuts, the garlic, 1 teaspoon of chopped chilies and ½ teaspoon of the salt and pound the mixture to a smooth paste. Stir in the vinegar with a wire whisk and, when it is thoroughly incorporated, add the olive oil in a slow, thin stream and beat vigorously until the sauce is thick. Taste for seasoning (you may add up to an additional teaspoon of chopped chili for a hotter sauce) and set the sauce aside.

Bring 3 cups of water and the remaining ½ teaspoon of salt to a boil in a heavy 2- to 3-quart saucepan. Drop in the cauliflower and cook briskly, uncovered, for 4 to 5 minutes, or until the flowerets are tender but still somewhat crisp to the bite. Drain the cauliflower in a large sieve or colander, then pat the flowerets completely dry with paper towels and drop them into a bowl. Pour the sauce over the cauliflower and toss together gently but thoroughly until all the flowerets are evenly coated. Cover the bowl tightly with foil or plastic wrap and refrigerate the *coliflor fria* for at least 2 hours, or until it is chilled.

Just before serving, toss the flowerets briefly and garnish the top with the chili strips and the remaining tablespoon of pine nuts.

Pinto Beans

To serve 6 to 8

2 cups (1 pound) dried pinto beans
6 cups water
1 medium-sized onion, peeled
1 medium-sized bay leaf
1 teaspoon salt

In a large sieve or colander, wash the pinto beans under running water until the draining water runs clear. Pick out and discard any beans that are broken or blemished. Drop the beans into a heavy 3- to 4-quart sauce-pan, add the water, onion and bay leaf, and bring to a boil over high heat. Reduce the heat to low, cover partially and simmer for 4 hours. Add the salt and continue to simmer for 30 minutes longer, or until the beans are tender but still intact.

Drain the beans in the sieve or colander, transfer them to a heated bowl and serve at once.

Trappers' Fruit

To make about 5 cups

3 cups (about 12 ounces) coarsely
   chopped dried apples
1 cup canned puréed pumpkin
½ cup dark brown sugar
¼ cup roasted sunflower seeds
¼ cup seedless raisins
¼ teaspoon coriander seeds
1 teaspoon salt
1 quart water

Combine the dried apples, pumpkin, brown sugar, sunflower seeds, raisins, coriander, salt and water in a heavy 3- to 4-quart casserole and mix well. Bring to a boil over high heat, reduce the heat to low, cover tightly and simmer for about 1½ hours, or until the apples are tender. Check the pan occasionally and, if the fruit seems dry, add more water ¼ cup at a time. Transfer the fruit to a bowl and cool to room temperature before serving. Trappers' fruit, so called because it was easy for Colorado fur trappers of the mid-19th Century to prepare, is served as an accompaniment to roasted and broiled meats.

Ginger Fruit Kabobs

To make 8 kabobs

8 tablespoons butter, cut into
  ½-inch bits
2 tablespoons sugar
1 teaspoon ground ginger
2 half-inch-thick orange slices, each
  cut crosswise into quarters
1 large firm apple, cored and cut
  lengthwise into 8 wedges
1 large banana, peeled and cut
  crosswise into 8 chunks
8 one-inch cubes fresh pineapple

Immerse eight individual Oriental bamboo skewers in water and soak them for at least an hour. Then light a layer of briquettes in a hibachi or charcoal broiler and let them burn until a white ash appears on the surface. Or preheat the broiler of the oven to its highest setting.

To prepare the basting syrup, combine the butter, sugar and ginger in a small pan and cook over low heat, stirring constantly until the butter melts and the sugar dissolves. Set the pan aside off the heat.

Thread an orange quarter, apple wedge, banana chunk and pineapple cube on each skewer, pushing the pieces of fruit close together. With a pastry brush, spread about 1 teaspoon of the basting syrup evenly over each fruit kabob.

Broil the kabobs about 3 inches from the heat for 2 minutes, turn them over and baste them with the remaining syrup. Continue to broil for 1 or 2 minutes longer, or until the kabobs are golden brown on all sides.

Arrange the kabobs attractively on a heated platter and serve them at once as an accompaniment to broiled steak or any roasted meat.

Chili Jelly

To make about 5 cups

½ pound fresh hot chilies, washed,
    stemmed and seeded *(caution:*
    see page 3)
2 medium-sized sweet bell peppers,
    washed, stemmed, seeded and
    deribbed
1½ cups cider vinegar
5 cups sugar
1 bottle liquid fruit pectin

Put the chilies and the bell peppers through the medium blade of a food grinder, or chop them very fine with a large sharp knife. You will need about ½ cup of each kind of pepper.

Combine the chilies, bell peppers and vinegar in a 1- to 2-quart enameled or stainless-steel saucepan and bring to a boil over high heat. Reduce the heat to low, cover tightly and simmer for 15 minutes.

Line a colander or sieve with a double thickness of dampened cheesecloth and set it over a large enameled pot. The bottom of the colander or sieve should be suspended above the bottom of the pot by at least 2 or 3 inches. Pour the chili mixture into the sieve and allow the liquid to drain through. (Do not squeeze the cloth or the finished jelly will be cloudy.)

When all the liquid has drained through, remove the sieve and discard the chilies and bell peppers. Add the sugar to the strained liquid and, stirring constantly, bring to a boil over high heat. Still stirring, boil briskly for 1 minute. Then remove the pan from the heat at once and stir in the pectin. Carefully skim off the surface foam with a large spoon. Ladle the amber-colored jelly into hot sterilized jars or jelly glasses, following the directions for home canning on page 2.

NOTE: Chili jelly is served with meats and fowl.

SEAFOOD

Shrimp and Chilies with Sherry Sauce

To serve 4 to 6

1½ pounds medium-sized
   uncooked shrimp (about 20 to 24
   to the pound), thoroughly
   defrosted if frozen
1 cup flour
1½ teaspoons salt
½ cup peanut oil
3 canned green *jalapeño* chilies,

drained, seeded and cut into
   matchlike strips 1 inch long and
   ⅛ inch wide *(caution: see note,
   page 3)*
½ cup pale dry sherry
6 cups freshly cooked rice made
   from 2 cups long-grain white rice
1 tablespoon finely chopped fresh
   parsley

Shell the shrimp. Devein them by making a shallow incision down their backs with a small sharp knife and lifting out the black or white intestinal vein with the point of the knife. Wash the shrimp in a sieve or colander set under cold running water, spread them on paper towels to drain, and pat them completely dry with fresh paper towels.

Combine the flour and salt in a paper bag, add the shrimp, and shake vigorously to coat them evenly. Remove the shrimp from the bag and shake each one to remove the excess flour. Lay the shrimp side by side on a sheet of wax paper.

In a heavy 10- to 12-inch skillet, heat the peanut oil over moderate heat until a light haze forms above it. Add the shrimp and, stirring constantly, cook for 4 to 5 minutes, until they are firm and delicately browned. Do not overcook the shrimp. Stir in the chilies, tip the skillet slightly and draw off the fat from the pan with a bulb baster.

Then warm the sherry in a small saucepan set over low heat. Carefully ignite the sherry with a long wooden match and pour it flaming over the shrimp and chilies. Gently slide the skillet back and forth over low heat until the flames die.

With a slotted spoon, arrange the shrimp and chilies attractively on a heated platter. Pour the sherry sauce over them. Mound the boiled rice in a bowl, sprinkle the top with the parsley and serve it at once as an accompaniment to the shrimp and chilies.

Abalone Steaks

To serve 2 or 4

12 tablespoons unsalted butter
  (1½ quarter-pound sticks), cut
  into ½-inch bits
½ cup flour
1 cup soft crumbs made from day-
  old homemade-type white bread,

pulverized in a blender
2 eggs, lightly beaten
4 four-ounce abalone steaks,
  thoroughly defrosted if frozen
1 teaspoon salt
¼ teaspoon ground white pepper
1 lemon, quartered

Clarify the butter in the following manner: Place the butter bits in a small heavy skillet and, stirring constantly, melt them over low heat. Do not let the butter brown.

Remove the skillet from the heat, then skim off the surface foam and discard it. Let the butter rest for a minute or so. Tipping the pan slightly, spoon the clear butter into a bowl and set it aside. Discard the milky solids at the bottom of the skillet.

Spread the flour on one piece of wax paper and the bread crumbs on another. Break the eggs into a shallow bowl and, with a wire whisk or a table fork, beat them only long enough to combine them.

Using the smooth side of a kitchen mallet or the flat side of a heavy cleaver, pound the abalone steaks to a uniform thickness of about ⅓ inch. Pat the steaks completely dry with paper towels and season them on both sides with salt and pepper.

Dip one steak at a time into the flour to coat it evenly, immerse it in the lightly beaten eggs, and turn it over and back in the bread crumbs. As they are coated, arrange the abalone steaks in one layer on wax paper. (At this stage, the steaks may be draped with wax paper and refrigerated for up to 1 hour if you like.)

Just before serving, heat 4 tablespoons of the clarified butter in a heavy 10- to 12-inch skillet over high heat. When the butter is very hot, add two of the steaks. Turning them with tongs, fry the steaks for 2 or 3 minutes on each side, or until the crust is golden brown. Transfer the fried abalone to a heated platter, add the remaining clarified butter to the skillet, and fry the other two steaks in the same fashion.

Garnish the platter with the lemon quarters and serve the abalone steaks at once.

Crab Louis

To serve 6

1½ cups freshly made mayonnaise (*page 29*), or substitute 1½ cups unsweetened bottled mayonnaise
¼ cup bottled chili sauce
3 tablespoons finely chopped scallions, including 2 inches of the green tops
3 tablespoons finely chopped sweet green bell peppers
1 tablespoon strained fresh lemon juice
1½ teaspoons Worcestershire sauce
4 drops Tabasco
½ teaspoon salt

1½ pounds (about 3 cups) freshly cooked or defrosted frozen crabmeat, preferably Dungeness, drained and thoroughly picked over to remove all bits of shell and cartilage, then cut into 1-inch pieces
3 large firm ripe avocados
2 heads bibb or Boston lettuce, separated into leaves, trimmed, washed and thoroughly chilled
2 medium-sized firm ripe tomatoes, washed, stemmed and each cut lengthwise into 6 wedges
3 hard-cooked eggs, cut lengthwise into quarters

Combine the mayonnaise, chili sauce, scallions, peppers, lemon juice, Worcestershire sauce, Tabasco and salt in a deep mixing bowl and stir with a wire whisk until the ingredients are well blended. Taste for seasoning, then add the crabmeat and toss it about gently with a spoon until the pieces are evenly coated.

Cut the avocados in half. With the tip of a small knife, loosen each seed and lift it out. Remove any brown tissuelike fibers clinging to the flesh. Strip off the skin with your fingers starting at the narrow stem end. (The dark-skinned variety does not peel easily; use a knife to pull the skin away, if necessary.)

To assemble the crab Louis, place the avocado halves on six individual serving plates and spoon the crab mixture into the cavities. Arrange the lettuce leaves in rings around the avocado, and garnish the leaves with the tomatoes and hard-cooked eggs. Serve at once.

Sole-and-Crab Mousse with Shrimp Sauce

To serve 6

FISH STOCK

1 pound fish trimmings: the heads, tails and bones of any firm white-fleshed fish

1 quart water

1 medium-sized onion, peeled and coarsely chopped

1 medium-sized bay leaf, crumbled

1 teaspoon salt

6 whole black peppercorns

½ pound raw shrimp

First prepare the fish stock in the following manner: Combine the fish trimmings and water in a 3- to 4-quart enameled or stainless-steel saucepan and bring to a boil over high heat, meanwhile skimming off the foam and scum as they rise to the surface. Add the chopped onion, bay leaf, salt and peppercorns, and reduce the heat to low. Simmer partially covered for 30 minutes, then strain the stock through a fine sieve set over a bowl, pressing down hard on the trimmings with the back of a spoon to extract all their juices before discarding the bones. Return the strained stock to the pan.

Meanwhile, shell the shrimp. Devein them by making a shallow incision down their backs with a small sharp knife and lifting out the black or white intestinal vein with the point of the knife.

Bring the fish stock to a simmer over moderate heat, drop in the shrimp and cook uncovered for 3 to 5 minutes, or until the shrimp are pink and firm. Do not overcook the shrimp. With a slotted spoon, transfer the shrimp to a plate. Reserve four whole shrimp to garnish the mousse, chop the rest into small dice and refrigerate them until needed. Bring the remaining fish stock to a boil and cook briskly, uncovered, until it is reduced to about 1 cup. Strain the stock through a fine sieve lined with a double thickness of cheesecloth and set over a bowl. Cool to room temperature, then refrigerate until you are ready to make the shrimp sauce.

MOUSSE

1 tablespoon vegetable oil

1 pound sole fillets, skinned and cut into 1-inch pieces

1 cup light cream

8 ounces frozen Alaskan king crabmeat, thoroughly defrosted and drained, then cut into 1-inch pieces

4 egg yolks

1 tablespoon finely grated onion

1 tablespoon strained fresh lemon juice

¼ teaspoon ground nutmeg, preferably freshly grated

¼ teaspoon ground white pepper

2 egg whites

½ cup heavy cream, chilled

To make the mousse, preheat the oven to 350°. With a pastry brush spread the vegetable oil over the bottom and sides of a heavy 6-cup fish mold or other decorative 6-cup mold. Invert the mold on paper towels to drain off the excess oil.

Place about one third of the sole and 2 tablespoons of light cream in the jar of an electric blender and blend at high speed for 30 seconds. Turn off the machine, scrape down the sides of the jar with a rubber spatula and blend again until the sole is a smooth purée. Transfer the puréed sole to a deep bowl and repeat two more times, adding 2 tablespoons of light cream to each batch.

Combine the crabmeat and the remaining 10 tablespoons of light cream in the blender, and purée it in similar fashion. With the spatula, scrape the crab purée over the sole purée. Add the 4 egg yolks and beat vigorously with a wooden spoon until the mixture is smooth. Stir in the grated onion, lemon juice, nutmeg and white pepper.

Beat the egg whites with a wire whisk or a rotary or electric beater until they are stiff enough to stand in unwavering peaks on the beater when it is lifted out of the bowl. In a chilled bowl, whip the heavy cream with the same beater until it stands in firm peaks.

With a rubber spatula, scoop the cream over the sole-and-crab mixture and fold them together gently but thoroughly. Add the egg whites and continue to fold until all the ingredients are well blended.

Spoon the mixture into the oiled mold and place it in a roasting pan set on the middle shelf of the oven. Pour enough boiling water into the pan to come halfway up the sides of the mold. Bake the mousse for 35 to 40 minutes, or until a knife inserted in the center comes out clean.

SHRIMP SAUCE
2 teaspoons cornstarch mixed with
   2 teaspoons water
2 egg yolks
½ cup light cream
2 tablespoons dry sherry

Meanwhile, complete the shrimp sauce. In a small saucepan, bring the reserved cup of fish stock to a simmer over low heat. Stirring constantly with a wire whisk, add the cornstarch mixture, and cook until the stock clears and thickens. Remove the pan from the heat.

In a heavy 1- to 1½-quart enameled saucepan, beat the 2 egg yolks with a wire whisk or a rotary or electric beater for a minute or so. Stirring constantly, add the ½ cup of light cream and then gradually pour in the hot fish stock in a slow, thin stream. Still stirring, cook the sauce over low heat for 2 or 3 minutes, but do not let it come near a boil or the egg yolks will curdle. Stir in the sherry and the reserved chopped shrimp, and taste for seasoning.

To unmold and serve the finished mousse, run a thin knife around the edges of the mold to loosen the sides. Place an inverted platter on top of the mold and, grasping platter and mold together firmly, turn them over. The mousse should slide out easily. Pour the sauce over the mousse, arrange the four reserved whole shrimp on top and serve at once.

Stuffed Flounder
To serve 4

½ pound raw shrimp
2 tablespoons butter, cut into small bits, plus 3 tablespoons butter, melted
3 tablespoons finely chopped shallots
2 tablespoons finely chopped celery
2 tablespoons finely chopped green bell peppers
¼ teaspoon curry powder
½ cup soft fresh crumbs made from homemade-type white bread, pulverized in a blender or finely shredded with a fork
1 tablespoon finely chopped fresh parsley
1½ teaspoons salt
¼ teaspoon freshly ground black pepper
Four 12- to 16-ounce flounder, cleaned, with the heads removed but with the tails intact

First make the stuffing in the following manner: Shell the shrimp. Devein them by making shallow incisions down their backs and lifting out the black or white intestinal veins with the point of the knife. Wash the shrimp under cold running water, pat them completely dry with paper towels and chop them into ¼-inch pieces.

In a heavy 8- to 10-inch skillet, melt the 2 tablespoons of butter bits over moderate heat. When the foam begins to subside, add the shallots, celery and bell peppers and, stirring frequently, cook for about 5 minutes, or until the vegetables are soft but not brown. Stir in the curry powder, then add the shrimp and stir the mixture over moderate heat for 1 to 2 minutes, or until the pieces of shrimp are firm and pink. Add the bread crumbs, the parsley, ½ teaspoon of the salt and the black pepper, and mix well. With a rubber spatula, scrape the entire contents of the skillet into a bowl. Taste for seasoning and set the stuffing aside to cool to room temperature.

Preheat the oven to 450°. With a pastry brush, spread 1 tablespoon of the melted butter evenly over the bottom of a shallow baking-serving dish large enough to hold the fish in one layer. Set aside.

Wash the fish under cold running water and pat them dry with paper towels. To prepare the flounder for stuffing, as shown above, place one at a time on its belly (light-colored side) on a cutting board. With a small sharp knife, make a 4- to 5-inch-long slit completely through the skin and top surface of flesh to the backbone of the fish, cutting from about 1 inch behind the head to within about 1 inch of the tail. With your fingers or the point of the knife, gently lift the top surface of the flesh away from the rows of small bones radiating from the backbone, to create pockets above and below the slit.

Sprinkle the remaining teaspoon of salt inside the pockets formed in the flounder. Then fill the pockets and the space between them with shrimp stuffing, dividing the mixture equally among the four fish.

Arrange the flounder side by side in the buttered dish and brush the tops with the remaining 2 tablespoons of melted butter. Bake in the middle of the oven for about 10 minutes, or until the fish feel firm when prodded gently with a finger. Serve the stuffed flounder at once, directly from the baking dish.

Sand Dab or Rex Sole en Papillote
To serve 4

3 tablespoons butter, cut into small bits, plus 4 tablespoons butter, softened
12 firm fresh mushroom caps, each about 1 inch in diameter, wiped with a dampened towel
8 four-ounce sand dab or rex sole fillets, skinned, or substitute
8 four-ounce skinned fillets of any firm white-fleshed fish
2 teaspoons salt
½ teaspoon ground white pepper
16 thin strips of boiled ham, ¼ inch thick, about 6 inches long and ½ inch wide
2 teaspoons finely cut fresh chives
2 teaspoons finely chopped fresh parsley

Preheat the oven to 450°. In a heavy 8- to 10-inch skillet, melt the butter bits over moderate heat. When the foam begins to subside, add the mushroom caps. Turning the mushrooms frequently with a slotted spoon, cook them for 3 to 4 minutes, or until they are delicately browned on both sides. Remove the skillet from the heat and set the mushroom caps aside.

With scissors cut four large hearts about 11 inches long and 15 inches wide out of parchment paper. Then, with a pastry brush, spread 1 tablespoon of the softened butter evenly over one side of each of the four paper hearts.

Pat the fish fillets completely dry with paper towels and season them with the salt and white pepper. To assemble each *papillote,* place two fillets on the buttered side of a paper heart and arrange four ham strips side by side over the fish. Sprinkle ½ teaspoon of the chives and ½ teaspoon of the parsley on the ham and set three of the mushroom caps on top.

Fold the paper over the fish so that the edges of the heart meet. Starting at the upper end of the fold, seal the edges by crimping them together at ½-inch intervals. Before crimping the point of the heart, open the seam slightly and insert a drinking straw. Blow through the straw to inflate the *papillote,* then quickly crimp the bottom point closed.

Arrange the *papillotes* side by side on a baking sheet and bake in the middle of the oven for 12 minutes. The paper should turn a golden brown. Serve the *papillotes* at once, opening the paper at the table.

Fillet of Rex Sole Santa Monica

To serve 4

2 tablespoons butter, softened, plus
   1 tablespoon butter, cut into
   ¼-inch bits
¼ cup finely chopped shallots
4 four-ounce skinned fillets of rex
   sole, or substitute any other
   4-ounce skinned sole or flounder
   fillets

¼ teaspoon crumbled dried
   rosemary
½ teaspoon salt
⅛ teaspoon ground white pepper
½ cup dry white wine
1 cup water
½ cup heavy cream
2 egg yolks

Preheat the oven to 350°. Brush the 2 tablespoons of softened butter over the bottom of a shallow baking dish large enough to hold the fillets comfortably and spread the shallots in the bottom of the dish.

Season the fillets on both sides with the rosemary, salt and pepper, and arrange them in one layer in the baking dish. Pour in the wine and water, and dot the top with the butter bits. Cover the dish with buttered wax paper, then poach the sole in the middle of the oven for 10 minutes, or until the fillets feel firm when prodded gently with a finger. Using a slotted spatula, transfer the fillets to a heated platter and drape the wax paper over them to keep them warm while you prepare the sauce.

Strain the poaching liquid through a fine sieve into a 1- to 1½-quart enameled or stainless-steel saucepan, pressing down hard on the shallots with the back of a spoon to extract all their juices before discarding them. Bring the liquid to a boil over high heat and cook briskly, uncovered, until it is reduced to about 1 cup. Add the cream and stir over high heat until the mixture thickens slightly. Then reduce the heat to low.

Beat the egg yolks lightly with a wire whisk, pour in about ½ cup of the cream mixture and whisk together thoroughly. Stirring the remaining cream mixture constantly with the whisk, pour in the yolk mixture in a slow, thin stream, then cook for 2 or 3 minutes, until the sauce thickens heavily. Do not let the sauce come near a boil or the yolks will curdle.

Taste the sauce for seasoning, pour it over the fish and serve at once.

Pan-fried Trout

To serve 4

Four 8- to 10-ounce rainbow, lake or mountain trout, cleaned but with heads and tails left on and thoroughly defrosted if frozen
2 teaspoons salt
¼ teaspoon freshly ground black pepper
½ cup yellow cornmeal
½ cup flour
3 tablespoons butter
6 tablespoons vegetable oil
1 lemon, cut into 4 or 8 wedges

Wash the trout briefly under cold running water and pat them completely dry inside and out with paper towels. Sprinkle the cavities and skins of the fish evenly with the salt and pepper. Mix the cornmeal and flour together in a large bowl.

In a heavy 12-inch skillet, melt the butter with the oil over moderate heat. When the foam begins to subside, roll each trout over in the cornmeal-and-flour mixture, shake off the excess coating, and place the fish in the skillet. Fry them for 4 to 5 minutes on each side, or until they are golden brown and crisp, and feel firm when prodded gently with a finger.

Arrange the trout attractively on a heated platter and serve them at once, accompanied by the lemon wedges.

San Francisco Fried Trout

To serve 4

Four 10- to 12-ounce trout, cleaned but with heads and tails left on, thoroughly defrosted if frozen
2 teaspoons salt
Freshly ground black pepper
1 cup unsifted flour
1 cup yellow cornmeal
2 eggs
1 cup vegetable oil
8 tablespoons butter, cut into bits
¼ cup strained fresh lime juice
2 tablespoons finely cut fresh chives
2 tablespoons finely chopped fresh parsley

Wash the trout under cold running water, pat them dry and season them inside and out with the salt and a few grindings of pepper. Spread the flour on one piece of wax paper and the cornmeal on a separate piece; break the eggs into a shallow bowl and beat them to a froth with a fork.

In a heavy 12-inch skillet, heat the oil over moderate heat until a light haze forms above it. Roll each trout in the flour, immerse it in the egg and then turn it about in the cornmeal to coat it evenly. Fry the trout in the hot oil, two at a time, for 4 to 5 minutes on each side, or until they are golden brown. Drain the trout briefly on paper towels, then place them on a heated platter.

Melt the butter over moderate heat in a separate skillet, stirring so that the bits melt without browning. Remove the pan from the heat, stir in the lime juice, chives and parsley, and taste for seasoning. Pour over the trout and serve at once.

Minted Trout

To serve 4

48 fresh leafy mint stalks, each 5 or 6 inches long, thoroughly washed and patted dry with paper towels	oil
	4 teaspoons salt
	Four 10- to 12-ounce trout, thoroughly defrosted if frozen
1 cup plus 1 tablespoon vegetable	8 slices lean bacon

Position the broiler pan and rack 4 inches below the source of heat, then preheat the broiler to its highest setting.

Drop 32 of the mint stalks into a deep bowl and bruise the leaves and stems with the back of a large spoon to release their flavor. Dribble 1 cup of the oil over the mint, add 2 teaspoons of the salt, and turn the stalks about with a spoon to coat them evenly.

Wash the trout briefly under cold running water and pat them dry inside and out with paper towels. Rub the cavities of the fish with the remaining 2 teaspoons of salt, dividing it evenly among them. Then stuff the cavities with the bruised mint stalks.

To wrap each fish, lay 2 bacon slices parallel to one another on a flat surface, spacing them about ½ inch apart. Place 2 of the remaining mint stalks at right angles to the bacon slices in the center of the row and lay a trout over the mint. Place 2 more mint stalks on top of the fish, lift the ends of the bacon slices and wrap them snugly around the mint and fish. Secure the bacon in place with wooden toothpicks. Repeat, arranging 2 of the mint stalks on both sides of each fish and holding the stalks in place with 2 slices of the bacon.

With a pastry brush, spread the remaining tablespoon of oil evenly over the broiler pan rack. Arrange the trout side by side on the rack and, turning them once with a metal spatula, broil for 4 to 5 minutes on each side, or until they feel firm when prodded gently with a finger.

Using a sharp knife or kitchen scissors, cut the bacon slices along the cavity of each fish and remove and discard the mint stuffing but leave the bacon and the whole mint stalks in place. Arrange the minted trout attractively on a large heated platter and serve them at once, garnished if you like by decoratively cut lemons.

Cioppino

Though the name cioppino sounds Italian, and the savory blend of tomatoes, garlic, wine and herbs that give this fish stew its zest is reminiscent of Mediterranean seafare, the word was actually coined in California—presumably by Italian fishermen who settled in the state. The stew itself bears a family resemblance to both the cacciucco alla livornese of Italy and the bouillabaisse of France. Like its European cousins, cioppino is made with whatever fish or seafood is available. Shrimp and even lobsters may be added; the mussels may be left out. Any firm white-fleshed fish, such as halibut or sea bass, may take the place of the cod. Live blue crabs may be substituted for the Dungeness variety, but blue crabs are small and should be cooked whole rather than cut up as are the larger Pacific crabs.

To serve 8

FISH STOCK

2 pounds fish trimmings: the heads, tails and bones of any firm white-fleshed fish
6 cups water
1 large onion, peeled and coarsely chopped
1 medium-sized bay leaf, crumbled
6 whole black peppercorns
1 teaspoon salt

To prepare the fish stock, combine the fish trimmings and water in a 4- to 5-quart enameled or stainless-steel pot and bring to a boil over high heat, skimming off the foam and scum that rise to the surface. Add the coarsely chopped onion and the bay leaf, peppercorns and 1 teaspoon of salt, reduce the heat to low, and simmer partially covered for 20 minutes.

Strain the contents of the pot through a fine sieve into a bowl, pressing down hard on the fish trimmings with the back of a spoon to extract all their juices. Measure and reserve 4 cups of the fish stock.

FISH STEW

¼ cup olive or vegetable oil
1 cup coarsely chopped onions
1 tablespoon finely chopped garlic
3 medium-sized firm ripe tomatoes, washed, coarsely chopped and puréed in a food mill, or substitute 1 cup canned puréed tomatoes
1 cup dry white wine
2 tablespoons finely chopped fresh
parsley
Two 1½-pound precooked Dungeness crabs, thoroughly defrosted if frozen
3 dozen large mussels in their shells
2 dozen small hard-shell clams in their shells
2 pounds fresh cod steaks, cut into 8 equal portions
½ teaspoon salt

Wash the pot, add the oil and heat it over moderate heat until a light haze forms above it. Add the cup of coarsely chopped onions and the garlic, and, stirring frequently, cook for about 5 minutes, until the onions are soft and translucent but not brown. Stir in the reserved stock, the tomato purée, wine and parsley, and bring to a boil over high heat. Reduce the heat and simmer partially covered for 15 minutes.

Meanwhile, prepare the crabs. Holding a crab tightly in one hand, lift off the top shell and discard it. Pull out the spongy gray lungs, or "dead man's fingers," from each side and scrape out the intestines in the center. Place the crab on its back and, with the point of a small sharp knife, pry off the pointed flap or apron. Cut away the head just behind the eyes. With a cleaver or heavy knife, cut the crab into quarters. Shell, clean and quarter the second crab in the same manner and set both aside on a plate.

Under cold running water, scrub the mussels and clams thoroughly with a stiff brush or soapless steel-mesh scouring pad, and remove the black ropelike tufts from the mussels. Season the cod on both sides with ½ teaspoon of salt. Set the mussels and clams and the cod aside on wax paper or plates.

To assemble the cioppino, arrange the pieces of crab in the bottom of a 6- to 8-quart enameled casserole. Lay the mussels and clams on top and pour in the tomato mixture. Bring to a boil over high heat, reduce the heat to low, cover tightly and cook for 10 minutes. Add the pieces of cod, cover the casserole again and continue to cook for 8 to 10 minutes longer. The cioppino is done when the mussel and clam shells have opened and the cod flakes easily when prodded gently with a fork. Discard any mussels or clams that remain closed.

Serve at once, directly from the casserole, or spoon the cod and shellfish into a large heated tureen and pour the broth over them.

POULTRY & GAME BIRDS

Grapefruit Duck

To serve 4 to 6

A 4½- to 5-pound duck
½ teaspoon salt
¼ teaspoon freshly ground black
  pepper
1 medium-sized onion, peeled and
quartered
¼ cup strained fresh grapefruit
  juice
¼ cup honey
2 tablespoons soy sauce

Preheat the oven to 450°. Wash the duck under cold running water and cut off the wing tips at the first joint. Pat the duck dry inside and out with paper towels. Rub the cavity of the duck with the salt and pepper and insert the onion quarters. Then truss the bird securely. For a crisper skin, prick the surface around the thighs, the back and the lower part of the breast with the point of a sharp knife.

Place the duck breast up on a rack set in a large shallow pan and roast for 20 minutes. Reduce the oven temperature to 350° and draw off the accumulated fat from the pan with a bulb baster or a large spoon. Turn the duck on one side and roast it for 30 minutes, then turn it on the other side and roast for 30 minutes longer.

Combine the grapefruit juice, honey and soy sauce in a bowl and mix well. Turn the duck breast up and, with a pastry brush, spread 2 or 3 tablespoons of the grapefruit mixture evenly over the bird. Roast the duck for 30 minutes longer, basting it twice more with about 3 tablespoons of the grapefruit mixture. Pierce the thigh of the bird with the point of a small sharp knife to make sure it is cooked through. The juice that trickles out should be clear yellow; if it is slightly tinged with pink, roast the bird for another 5 to 10 minutes.

Transfer the duck to a heated platter and let it rest for about 10 minutes for easier carving.

Lemon Chicken

To serve 4

1 lemon	½ teaspoon paprika
1½ teaspoons salt	½ cup vegetable oil
A 2½- to 3-pound chicken, cut into 8 serving pieces	1 cup chicken stock, fresh or canned
	2 tablespoons dark brown sugar
½ cup flour	½ teaspoon Angostura bitters

Preheat the oven to 375°. With a sharp knife, cut the lemon in half cross-wise and slice one half into paper-thin rounds. Set the lemon slices aside and squeeze the juice of the remaining lemon half into a deep bowl. Stir the salt into the lemon juice.

Pat the pieces of chicken completely dry, drop them into the bowl with the lemon juice and salt, and turn the pieces about with a spoon to moisten them evenly. Combine the flour and paprika in a large paper bag, add two or three pieces of chicken at a time to the bag, and shake them until they are lightly covered with the flour mixture. Remove the chicken from the bag and shake off the excess flour.

In a heavy 10- to 12-inch skillet, heat the oil over moderate heat until a light haze forms above it. Brown three or four pieces of chicken at a time in the hot oil, starting the pieces skin side down and turning them frequently with tongs so that they color richly and evenly all over without burning. As they brown, arrange the pieces of chicken in one layer in a large baking dish equipped with a tight-fitting cover.

Pour off the fat remaining in the skillet and in its place add the chicken stock. Bring to a boil over high heat, meanwhile scraping in the browned particles that cling to the bottom and sides of the pan. Stir in the brown sugar and, when it is dissolved, remove the skillet from the heat and add the bitters. Pour the stock mixture over the chicken and arrange the lemon slices on top.

Cover the dish tightly and bake the chicken in the middle of the oven for about 30 minutes, or until it is tender and shows no resistance when pierced deeply with the point of a small sharp knife. With tongs, transfer the chicken to a heated platter. Discard the lemon slices and strain the gravy remaining in the baking dish through a fine sieve into a bowl. With a spoon, skim as much fat as possible from the surface of the gravy. Taste for seasoning, pour the gravy over the chicken and serve at once.

Chicken-Jalapeño Pancakes
To serve 4 or 8

PANCAKES

½ cup unsifted flour
1 whole egg plus 1 egg yolk
⅔ cup milk

6 tablespoons butter, melted and
  cooled
¼ teaspoon salt

First prepare the pancakes in the following manner: Combine the ½ cup of flour, the whole egg, egg yolk, milk, 3 tablespoons of the cooled melted butter and the ¼ teaspoon of salt in the jar of an electric blender. Blend at high speed for 30 seconds, then turn off the machine. Scrape down the sides of the jar with a rubber spatula and blend again until the batter is smooth. Place the blender jar in the refrigerator and let the batter rest for an hour or so before using it.

Heat a 6-inch crêpe pan or skillet over high heat until a drop of water flicked into it splutters and evaporates instantly. Using a pastry brush, lightly grease the bottom and sides of the pan with a little of the remaining 3 tablespoons of melted butter. Pour in about 2 tablespoons of batter and tip the pan so that the batter quickly covers the bottom; the batter should cling to the pan and begin to firm up immediately.

At once tilt the pan over the blender jar and pour off any excess batter. The finished pancake should be no more than ⅟₁₆ inch thick; dilute the batter by beating in drops of water if necessary. Cook the pancake for a minute or so, until a rim of brown shows around the edge. Turn it over with a spatula and cook the other side for a minute longer. Slide the cake onto a plate. Brush butter on the skillet again and proceed with the rest of the pancakes. When finished, you will have eight pancakes.

(The pancakes may be made hours or even days ahead of time, stacked and covered tightly and kept in the refrigerator or freezer until you are ready to use them. If you do this, let the pancakes return to room temperature before attempting to separate them.)

FILLING

2 one-pound chicken breasts,
  skinned and boned
½ teaspoon salt
¼ teaspoon ground white pepper
2 tablespoons butter
3 tablespoons flour
1 cup chicken stock, fresh or canned

1 cup heavy cream
4 canned *jalapeño* chilies, each
  about 2 inches long, rinsed,
  halved, seeded and finely
  chopped *(caution: see note, page 3)*
2 tablespoons butter, softened
1 cup finely grated Swiss cheese

To prepare the filling, pat the chicken breasts completely dry with paper towels and season them on all sides with ½ teaspoon of salt and the white pepper. In a heavy 10-inch skillet, melt 2 tablespoons of butter over moderate heat. When the foam begins to subside, add the chicken breasts and, with tongs, turn them about in the butter to coat them evenly. Reduce the heat to its lowest setting and cover the skillet tightly. Turning the breasts once or twice, cook them until the meat is opaque and feels firm when prodded with a finger. Transfer the breasts to a plate and, with a sharp knife, cut them in ¼-inch dice. Set aside.

Add 3 tablespoons of flour to the fat remaining in the skillet and mix well. Stirring constantly with a wire whisk, pour in the chicken stock in a slow, thin stream and cook over high heat until the sauce comes to a boil, thickens heavily and is smooth. Still whisking constantly, add the cream and cook briskly until the sauce is reduced to about 1½ cups. Pour the sauce into a bowl, add the chicken dice and the chilies, and mix the filling well. Taste for seasoning.

Preheat the oven to 325°. With a pastry brush, spread the 2 tablespoons of softened butter evenly over the bottom and sides of a 14-by-6-by-2-inch baking-serving dish. Spoon about ¼ cup of the chicken filling onto the lower third of each pancake and roll it up; do not tuck in the ends. Arrange the pancakes side by side in the baking dish and sprinkle them with the grated cheese.

Bake in the upper third of the oven for 10 minutes, then increase the oven temperature to 500°. Continue baking for about 5 minutes longer, or until the cheese is melted and lightly browned. Serve the chicken-*jalapeño* pancakes at once, directly from the baking dish.

Chicken Raphael Weill

Chicken Raphael Weill is named after a San Francisco businessman who was an inspired amateur chef.

To serve 4 to 6

A 3-pound chicken, cut into 6 or
  8 serving pieces
½ teaspoon salt
¼ teaspoon ground white pepper
4 tablespoons butter
2 tablespoons finely chopped
  shallots
¼ cup brandy

½ cup chicken stock, fresh or
  canned
½ cup dry white wine
2 fresh parsley sprigs and
  ½ teaspoon dried tarragon,
  wrapped together in cheesecloth
1½ cups heavy cream
2 tablespoons dry sherry
3 egg yolks

Pat the pieces of chicken dry with paper towels and season them on all sides with the salt and white pepper. In a heavy 12-inch skillet, melt the butter over moderate heat. Add the shallots and stir for 2 or 3 minutes, until they are soft but not brown. Add the chicken and turn the pieces with tongs until they become opaque and firm, and are a pale golden color. Regulate the heat if necessary so that the chicken does not brown.

Warm the brandy in a small pan, ignite it and, as it flames, pour it over the chicken. Slide the skillet back and forth gently until the flames die, then add the stock, the wine and the cheesecloth bag of parsley and tarragon. Bring to a boil over high heat and reduce the heat to low. Simmer partially covered for 25 to 30 minutes, or until the chicken is tender and shows no resistance when pierced deeply with the point of a small sharp knife. With tongs, transfer the chicken to a plate.

Pick the wrapped herbs out of the skillet and discard them, and add the cream and sherry. Stirring constantly, bring to a boil over high heat and cook briskly, uncovered, until the mixture has been reduced to about 2 cups. Reduce the heat to its lowest setting.

Beat the egg yolks lightly with a wire whisk, ladle about ½ cup of the cream mixture into the yolks and mix well. Stirring constantly with the whisk, pour the yolk mixture into the skillet in a slow, thin stream and cook for 2 or 3 minutes, until the sauce thickens heavily and is smooth. Do not let the sauce come anywhere near a boil or the yolks will curdle. Taste for seasoning, then return the chicken to the skillet. Turning the pieces frequently, simmer for a minute to heat the chicken through.

Arrange the pieces of chicken attractively on a heated platter, pour the sauce over them and serve at once.

Turkey Chili

To serve 12 to 15

½ pound dried *ancho* chilies
1 quart boiling water
¼ cup vegetable oil
14 pounds turkey breasts or legs, or
  a combination of breasts and legs,
  thoroughly defrosted if frozen,
  skinned, boned and cut into
  ¼-inch pieces (about 14 cups)
1 cup chili powder
1½ tablespoons ground cumin

1 quart tomato purée
1 cup finely chopped onions
4 teaspoons finely chopped garlic
1 tablespoon salt
½ cup yellow cornmeal
12 cups freshly cooked pinto beans,
  made from 4 cups dried beans
  (page 40)
12 cups freshly cooked rice, made
  from 3 cups long-grain white rice

Under cold running water, pull the stems off the *ancho* chilies, then tear the chilies in half and brush out their seeds. Crumble the chilies coarsely, drop them into a bowl, and pour the boiling water over them. Let the chilies soak for at least 30 minutes, then strain the soaking liquid through a sieve set over a bowl. Place the chilies and 1 cup of the soaking liquid in the jar of an electric blender and blend at high speed for 30 seconds. Turn off the machine, scrape down the sides of the jar with a rubber spatula and blend again until the mixture is a smooth purée. Set the puréed chilies and the remaining soaking liquid aside.

In a heavy 7- to 8-quart casserole, heat the oil over moderate heat until a light haze forms above it. Add the turkey meat and, stirring constantly, cook until the pieces of meat are firm but not brown. Add the chili powder and cumin, and continue to stir for 2 or 3 minutes.

Stir in the puréed chilies, the reserved soaking liquid, the tomato purée, onions, garlic and salt, and mix well. Bring to a boil over high heat, reduce the heat to low, and simmer partially covered for about 30 minutes, or until the turkey is tender. Stirring the mixture constantly, pour in the cornmeal in a slow stream and cook over high heat until the chili comes to a boil and thickens lightly.

Taste for seasoning and serve at once, directly from the casserole or from a heated bowl. Mound the pinto beans and rice in separate bowls and present them with the chili.

Quail in Lemon-Wine Sauce

To serve 6

3 large lemons
6 four-ounce oven-ready quail,
  thoroughly defrosted if frozen
1 teaspoon salt
½ teaspoon freshly ground black
  pepper
½ cup flour

3 tablespoons butter
1 tablespoon vegetable oil
½ cup finely chopped onions
½ cup dry white wine
½ cup water
½ cup heavy cream
2 tablespoons finely chopped fresh
  parsley

With a small sharp knife, remove the skin from two of the lemons without cutting into the bitter white pith beneath it. Cut the peel into strips about ⅛ inch wide, drop the strips into enough boiling water to cover them completely and boil briskly for 2 minutes. With a slotted spoon, transfer the strips of lemon peel to paper towels to drain. Cut the remaining lemon crosswise into four or six rounds and set aside.

Wash the quail under cold running water and pat them dry with paper towels. Season them inside and out with salt and pepper, twist the wings behind the backs and truss the birds securely. Roll one at a time in the flour to coat it evenly and vigorously shake off the excess flour.

In a heavy casserole large enough to hold the quail in one layer, melt the butter with the oil over moderate heat. When the foam begins to subside, brown the birds in the hot fat, two or three at a time. Turn them frequently with tongs and regulate the heat so that they color richly and evenly without burning. As they brown, transfer them to a plate.

Add the onions to the fat remaining in the casserole and cook for about 5 minutes, stirring frequently until they are soft and translucent but not brown. Pour in the wine and water, and bring to a boil, meanwhile scraping in the brown particles that cling to the bottom and sides of the pan. Return the quail and the liquid that has accumulated around them to the casserole, cover tightly and simmer over low heat for 30 to 40 minutes. To test for doneness, pierce a thigh with the point of a small sharp knife. The juice that trickles out should be pale yellow; if it is still tinged with pink, braise the quail for another 5 to 10 minutes. Transfer the birds to a heated platter and drape them loosely with foil to keep them warm while you prepare the sauce.

Strain the braising liquid through a fine sieve set over a small heavy saucepan, pressing down hard on the onions with the back of a spoon to extract all their juices before discarding the pulp. Add the cream and, stirring frequently, cook the sauce over moderate heat until it thickens slightly and is reduced to about 1 cup. Stir in the reserved strips of lemon peel and taste for seasoning. Pour the sauce over the quail, then sprinkle the parsley in a ring around the outside edge of each lemon slice. Arrange the slices attractively on the platter and serve the quail at once.

NOTE: Where doves are available, they may be substituted for quail.

Spit-roasted Quail with Grapes

To serve 6

12 preserved grape leaves
6 oven-ready quail, about 4 ounces
  each, thoroughly defrosted if
  frozen

1 teaspoon salt
½ teaspoon freshly ground black
  pepper
2 dozen large green grapes
6 bacon slices

Light a 1- to 2-inch-thick layer of briquettes in a charcoal grill equipped with a rotating spit and let the briquettes burn until white ash appears on the surface.

Meanwhile, bring 2 quarts of water to a boil in a large pot. Drop in the grape leaves and immediately turn off the heat. Let the leaves soak for 1 minute, drain, then plunge them into a bowl of cold water to cool them quickly. Gently separate the leaves and spread them flat and side by side on paper towels to drain.

With a large sharp knife, cut the necks off the quail. Wash the birds briefly under cold running water and dry them thoroughly with paper towels. Season the quail inside and out with the salt and pepper. Slice the grapes almost in half lengthwise and pick out the seeds. Then stuff three or four grapes into the cavity of each bird. Twist the wings behind the backs of the quails and truss them securely.

Place one quail at a time in the center of a grape leaf and bring the ends of the leaf up around the bird. Drape a second grape leaf over the top of the quail and tuck the ends underneath the bird. Wrap a slice of bacon tightly around the middle of each bird.

Thread the quail on the spit side by side, securing them with the sliding prongs. Fit the spit into place above the coals, and roast the birds for 30 to 40 minutes. To test for doneness, pierce a thigh with the point of a small sharp knife. The juice that trickles out should be pale yellow; if it is still tinged with pink, roast the quail for another 5 to 10 minutes.

To serve, remove the spit from the grill, unscrew the prongs and slide the quail off the spit onto a heated platter.

NOTE: Mourning doves may be substituted for the quail.

Spit-roasted Wild Ducks with Olives
To serve 4

Two 1½- to 2-pound oven-ready
    wild ducks, with necks, gizzards
    and hearts coarsely chopped and
    reserved
1 teaspoon salt
3 tablespoons butter
1 tablespoon olive oil

½ cup finely chopped onions
2 tablespoons flour
1½ cups chicken stock, fresh or
    canned
¼ cup finely chopped pitted green
    olives
12 whole pitted green olives

Light a 1- to 2-inch-thick layer of briquettes in a charcoal grill equipped with a rotating spit. Let the coals burn until white ash appears on the surface. (This may take as long as an hour.)

Meanwhile, wash the ducks briefly under cold running water and pat them dry with paper towels. Season the ducks inside and out with the salt, then secure the neck skin to the back of each bird with a small skewer and truss the ducks securely. String the ducks lengthwise end to end on the spit and anchor them in place with the sliding prongs.

Fit the spit into place above the coals and roast the birds for 1½ to 2 hours. To test for doneness, pierce a thigh with the point of a small sharp knife. The juice that trickles out should be pale yellow; if it is still tinged with pink, roast the ducks for another 5 to 10 minutes.

Meanwhile, prepare the sauce. In a heavy 10- to 12-inch skillet, melt the butter in the oil over moderate heat. When the foam begins to subside, add the chopped necks, gizzards and hearts. Fry the duck giblets for 4 or 5 minutes, stirring them frequently and regulating the heat so that the pieces brown richly and evenly without burning. Add the onions and, when they color lightly, mix in the flour. Then, stirring constantly, pour in the stock in a slow, thin stream and cook over high heat until the sauce comes to a boil and thickens slightly. Add the chopped olives, reduce the heat to low, and simmer the sauce partially covered for 30 minutes.

Strain the sauce through a fine sieve set over a small saucepan, pressing down hard on the giblets and olives with the back of a spoon to extract all their juices before discarding the pulp and neck bones. Skim as much fat as possible from the surface of the sauce and taste for seasoning.

To serve, remove the spit from the grill, unscrew the prongs and slide the ducks onto a heated platter. Remove the trussing strings, and garnish the birds with the whole olives. Reheat the sauce over low heat if necessary and serve it from a gravy boat or sauce bowl.

Hearst Ranch Squab

To serve 4

6 tablespoons butter, cut into bits, plus 6 tablespoons butter, melted
7 or 8 slices homemade-type white bread, trimmed of all crusts and cut into ¼-inch cubes (about 3 cups)
½ cup finely chopped onions
1½ teaspoons finely chopped garlic
¾ cup freshly grated imported Parmesan cheese
1 tablespoon finely chopped fresh parsley
¼ teaspoon crumbled dried marjoram
1½ teaspoons salt
⅛ teaspoon ground white pepper
4 one-pound oven-ready squab
Parsley sprigs or watercress for garnish

First prepare the stuffing in the following manner: Preheat the oven to 400°. In a heavy 8- to 10-inch skillet, melt 4 tablespoons of the butter bits over moderate heat. When the foam begins to subside, drop in the bread cubes and, stirring frequently, fry them until they are golden brown on all sides. Transfer the bread cubes to a mixing bowl. In the skillet melt the remaining 2 tablespoons of butter bits. When the foam subsides, add the onions and garlic, and stir over moderate heat for 5 minutes, or until the onions are soft and translucent but not brown.

With a rubber spatula, scrape the entire contents of the skillet over the bread cubes. Mix well, then stir in the grated cheese, chopped parsley, marjoram, ½ teaspoon of the salt and the white pepper. Taste the stuffing for seasoning.

Wash the squab briefly under cold running water and pat them completely dry inside and out with paper towels. Season the cavities of the birds with the remaining teaspoon of salt, and fill the cavities with the stuffing, dividing it equally among them. Sew the openings securely with white thread, then truss the bird securely.

Place the birds side by side on a rack set in a shallow roasting pan and, using a pastry brush, coat the squab evenly with 2 tablespoons of the melted butter. Roast in the middle of the oven for about 40 minutes, brushing the birds from time to time with the remaining melted butter and the fat that will accumulate in the bottom of the pan.

To test for doneness, pierce the thighs of the birds with the point of a small sharp knife. The juice that trickles out should be a clear yellow; if it is tinged with pink, roast the squab for 5 or 10 minutes longer.

Arrange the squab attractively on a heated platter, garnish them with parsley or watercress and serve at once.

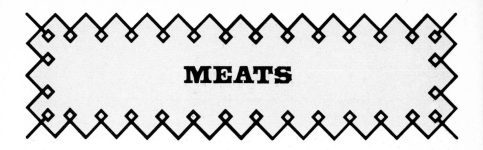

MEATS

Broiled Ham Steak with Cantaloupe

To serve 4

½ pound butter, cut into ½-inch
  bits
½ cup finely chopped bottled
  chutney
2 teaspoons curry powder
1 tablespoon vegetable oil

A 2-pound center-cut ham steak, cut
  about ¾ inch thick and trimmed
  of all but ⅛ inch of fat
1 large firm ripe cantaloupe, cut
  lengthwise into 8 equal wedges
  and peeled

Light a layer of briquettes in a charcoal grill and let them burn until white ash appears on the surface. Or preheat the broiler of your stove to its highest setting.

Meanwhile, in a small saucepan, melt the butter over moderate heat, stirring so that it melts evenly without browning. Remove the pan from the heat, add the chutney and curry powder, and mix well.

With a pastry brush, spread the vegetable oil evenly over the grill of the barbecue or the rack of the broiling pan. Place the ham steak on the grill or rack, and brush the top with about ⅓ cup of the chutney mixture. Broil the ham steak for about 15 minutes, turning it over every 5 minutes with kitchen tongs and brushing it each time with about ⅓ cup of the chutney mixture. When the ham steak is richly browned on both sides, transfer it to a heated platter.

Arrange the wedges of cantaloupe in one layer on the grill or broiling-pan rack, brush them with about half of the remaining chutney mixture and broil them for 1 or 2 minutes. Turn the wedges over, coat them with the rest of the mixture and broil for about 1 minute longer, or until they are richly colored.

Serve the ham steak at once, surrounded on the platter by the broiled cantaloupe wedges.

Vineyard Leg of Lamb

This method of roasting lamb is a fairly complicated one. The surface of the finished roast, however, takes on an unusually rich chestnut-brown color and is well worth the extra effort.

To serve 6 to 8

A 5- to 6-pound leg of lamb, trimmed of excess fat and with the fell (the parchmentlike covering) removed
2 medium-sized garlic cloves, peeled and cut lengthwise into paper-thin slivers

1 cup brandy
1 teaspoon ground cumin
1½ tablespoons salt
2 teaspoons freshly ground black pepper
¼ cup dry sherry
¼ cup dry white wine
Sprigs of watercress for garnish

With the point of a small sharp knife, cut a dozen or more 1-inch-deep slits all over the surface of the leg of lamb and insert a sliver of garlic into each slit. Cut a double thickness of cheesecloth about 16 inches wide and 18 to 20 inches long and drench it thoroughly with ½ cup of the brandy. Wrap the cheesecloth around the leg of lamb and cover it tightly with plastic wrap to prevent the brandy from evaporating. Set the lamb aside to marinate at room temperature for about 2 hours.

Preheat the oven to 450°. Mix the cumin, salt and pepper together in a small bowl, and combine the sherry and white wine in another bowl. Unwrap the lamb and place the leg, fat side up, on a rack in a shallow roasting pan. Press the cumin mixture into the surface of the lamb, coating the meat with the spices as evenly as possible. For the most predictable results, insert a meat thermometer 2 inches into the thickest part of the leg, being careful not to touch the bone.

Roast the lamb in the middle of the oven for 20 minutes. Then reduce the heat to 350° and baste with a tablespoon or so of the wine mixture. Continue to roast 40 to 60 minutes longer, or until the leg is cooked to your taste, basting two or three more times with the remaining wine mixture. A meat thermometer will register 130° when the lamb is rare, 140° when medium and 150° when well done.

Transfer the lamb to a heated platter and let the roast rest for 15 minutes for easier carving. Just before serving, warm the remaining ½ cup of brandy in a small saucepan. Ignite the brandy with a match and pour it flaming over the lamb. When the flame dies, garnish the platter with sprigs of watercress and serve at once.

Lamb and Limas

To serve 6 to 8

6 cups water

1 pound (about 2½ cups) dried Lima beans

3 pounds lean boneless lamb shoulder, trimmed of excess fat and cut into 1-inch cubes

2 teaspoons salt

½ teaspoon freshly ground black pepper

¼ cup flour

¼ cup vegetable oil

1½ teaspoons finely chopped garlic

2 to 3 cups chicken stock, fresh or canned

1 teaspoon crumbled dried oregano

¼ teaspoon crumbled dried thyme

¼ teaspoon crumbled dried rosemary

2 medium-sized carrots, scraped and sliced crosswise into ¼-inch-thick rounds

6 to 8 white onions, each about 1 inch in diameter, peeled

2 medium-sized celery stalks, trimmed of all leaves and cut crosswise into ¼-inch-thick slices

2 tablespoons butter

¼ pound firm fresh small mushrooms, trimmed and wiped with a dampened towel

In a 3- to 4-quart saucepan, bring the 6 cups of water to a boil over high heat. Drop in the Lima beans, boil briskly for 2 minutes, then turn off the heat. Let the beans soak for about 1 hour.

Meanwhile, pat the cubes of lamb completely dry with paper towels and season the meat with the salt and pepper. Roll the cubes in the flour to coat them on all sides, then vigorously shake off the excess flour.

In a heavy 7- to 8-quart casserole, heat the oil over moderate heat until a light haze forms above it. Brown five or six of the lamb cubes at a time, turning them frequently with a slotted spoon and regulating the heat so that they color deeply and evenly without burning. As they brown, transfer the lamb cubes to a plate.

Pour off all but about 2 tablespoons of the fat remaining in the casserole, add the garlic and stir over moderate heat for a minute or so. Then pour in 2 cups of chicken stock and bring to a boil over high heat, meanwhile scraping in the brown particles that cling to the bottom and sides of the pot. Add the oregano, thyme and rosemary, and return the lamb and the liquid that has accumulated around it to the casserole. Reduce the heat to low, cover the casserole and simmer for 30 minutes.

Drain the Lima beans in a sieve set over a bowl. Measure the bean-soaking liquid and add enough chicken stock to make 2 cups. Add the bean liquid, the beans and the carrots to the casserole, and simmer partially covered for 30 minutes longer. Stir in the onions and celery and simmer for 15 minutes, until the lamb and vegetables are tender but still intact.

In the meantime, melt the butter over moderate heat in a small heavy skillet. When the foam begins to subside, add the mushrooms. Stirring frequently, cook for about 10 minutes, or until the liquid that accumulates in the pan has completely evaporated. Do not let the mushrooms brown.

Stir the mushrooms into the simmering lamb mixture, and cook for 2 or 3 minutes more. Taste for seasoning. Serve the lamb and Limas at once, directly from the casserole.

Chuletas de Carnero con Piñones
LAMB CHOPS WITH PINE NUTS

To serve 4

½ cup pine nuts *(pignolia)*
3 large garlic cloves, peeled and coarsely chopped
2 dried hot red chilies, each about 1 inch long, stemmed, seeded and coarsely crumbled *(caution: see note, page 3)*

½ teaspoon salt
2 tablespoons distilled white vinegar
1 teaspoon sugar
A 6-ounce can tomato paste
¾ cup plus 1 tablespoon olive oil
4 lean shoulder lamb chops, each cut about 1 inch thick

Place the pine nuts in a small ungreased skillet and, stirring frequently, toast them over moderate heat for 5 to 10 minutes, or until they are golden brown. Transfer ¼ cup of the nuts to a large mortar or small heavy bowl and set the rest aside.

With a pestle or the back of a spoon, pulverize the ¼ cup of pine nuts. Add the garlic, chilies and salt and pound the mixture to a smooth paste. Stir in the vinegar and sugar, then add the tomato paste and, when it is well incorporated, beat in ¾ cup of the olive oil, 2 tablespoons at a time. Set the tomato sauce aside.

Set the broiler pan and rack 4 inches from the heat and preheat the broiler to its highest setting. With a pastry brush, spread the remaining tablespoon of olive oil over the broiler pan rack. Place the lamb chops on the rack and brush each one with a heaping tablespoon of the sauce. Broil the chops for 5 to 6 minutes, turn them over, and coat the top of each one with another heaping tablespoon of sauce. Broil for 5 to 6 minutes longer, or until the lamb chops are done to your taste.

Arrange the lamb chops attractively on a heated platter and scatter the reserved whole pine nuts over them. Warm the tomato sauce briefly over low heat and present it separately in a small bowl.

Lamb and Broccoli St. Francis

To serve 4 to 6

3 pounds lean boneless lamb,
    trimmed of excess fat and cut into
    1-inch cubes
1 teaspoon salt
½ teaspoon freshly ground black
    pepper
6 tablespoons vegetable oil
2 cups finely chopped onions

1 teaspoon finely chopped garlic
2 cups water
1 pound firm fresh brocolli,
    stemmed, washed and separated
    into small flowerets
3 egg yolks
3 tablespoons flour
½ cup strained fresh lemon juice

This richly sauced braised-lamb-and-broccoli stew is named for the St. Francis Hotel in San Francisco.

Pat the lamb cubes completely dry with paper towels and season them with the salt and pepper.

In a heavy 5- to 6-quart casserole, heat 4 tablespoons of the oil over moderate heat until a light haze forms above it. Brown the lamb, seven or eight pieces at a time, turning the cubes about frequently with tongs and regulating the heat so that they color richly and evenly on all sides without burning. As they brown, transfer the cubes of lamb to a plate.

Add the remaining 2 tablespoons of oil to the casserole, then drop in the onions and garlic. Stirring frequently, cook over moderate heat for about 5 minutes, or until the onions are soft and translucent but not brown. Pour in the water and bring the mixture to a boil over high heat, meanwhile scraping in the brown particles clinging to the bottom and sides of the pot.

Return the lamb and the liquid that has accumulated around it to the casserole. Stir well, reduce the heat to low and simmer partially covered for 45 minutes. Stir in the broccoli, cover the casserole partially again and simmer for 15 minutes more, or until the lamb shows no resistance when pierced deeply with the point of a small sharp knife. Reduce the heat to its lowest setting.

Combine the egg yolks and flour in a small bowl and beat with a wire whisk until the mixture is smooth. Whisk in the lemon juice, then beat in about ½ cup of the lamb-braising liquid. Stirring the lamb and broccoli constantly with a wooden spoon, pour in the egg-yolk mixture in a slow, thin stream and cook for 2 or 3 minutes, until the sauce thickens heavily and is smooth. Do not let the sauce come anywhere near a boil or the egg yolks will curdle.

Taste for seasoning and serve at once, directly from the casserole or from a deep heated platter.

Carne Santa Fe
SPICED BRAISED BEEF

To serve 4 to 6

2 pounds lean top round of beef,
   cut ½ inch thick and trimmed
   of excess fat
½ cup flour
3 tablespoons vegetable oil
1 medium-sized onion, peeled and
   sliced crosswise into ¼-inch-
   thick rounds
A 1-pound can tomatoes, drained
   and coarsely chopped, with the
   liquid reserved

A 4-ounce can green chilies (not
   the *jalapeño* variety), drained
   and coarsely chopped
½ cup dry red wine
1 tablespoon dark brown sugar
1 teaspoon crumbled dried mint
½ teaspoon fennel seeds, crushed
   with a mortar and pestle or
   wrapped in a kitchen towel and
   crushed with a kitchen mallet or
   the side of a cleaver
½ teaspoon salt

Pat the beef completely dry with paper towels and sprinkle it evenly on both sides with the flour. With a kitchen mallet or the flat of a cleaver, pound the beef to a uniform thickness of about ¼ inch, turning the meat over from time to time. Then shake the beef vigorously to remove the excess flour.

In a heavy 12-inch skillet, heat the oil over moderate heat until a light haze forms above it. Brown the beef in the hot oil, turning it occasionally with tongs and regulating the heat so that the meat colors richly and evenly without burning. Transfer the beef to a platter and set it aside.

Add the onion slices to the fat remaining in the skillet and, stirring frequently, cook for about 5 minutes, until they are soft and translucent but not brown. Stir in the tomatoes, chilies, wine, brown sugar, mint, fennel and salt, and bring to a boil over high heat. Return the beef and the liquid that has accumulated around it to the skillet and spoon the tomato mixture over it. Reduce the heat to low, cover the pan partially and simmer for about 1 hour, or until the beef shows no resistance when pierced deeply with the point of a small sharp knife.

Transfer the beef to a heated platter and taste the braising sauce for seasoning. If the sauce seems thin, boil it briskly over high heat, stirring all the while. When the sauce reaches the consistency you desire, pour it over the beef. Serve the *carne Santa Fe* at once.

Barbecued Spareribs with Red Sauce

To serve 4 to 6

½ cup vegetable oil
3 cups coarsely chopped onions
1 tablespoon finely chopped garlic
A 1-pound can tomatoes, drained
    and coarsely chopped with the
    liquid reserved
1 cup canned tomato purée
¼ cup coarsely chopped fresh hot

red chilies including the seeds
    (caution: see note, page 3)
2 tablespoons dry mustard
2 tablespoons sugar
1 tablespoon distilled white vinegar
1½ teaspoons salt
4 pounds spareribs, in 4 pieces,
    trimmed of excess fat

First prepare the red sauce in the following manner: In a heavy 10- to 12-inch skillet, heat the vegetable oil over moderate heat. Add the onions and garlic and, stirring frequently, cook for about 5 minutes, or until they are soft and translucent but not brown. Stir in the tomatoes and their liquid, the tomato purée, chilies, mustard, sugar, vinegar and salt, and bring to a boil over high heat. Cook briskly, uncovered, until the sauce is thick enough to hold its shape almost solidly in the spoon. Remove the pan from the heat and taste the red sauce for seasoning. Set it aside.

To barbecue the ribs, light a 2-inch-thick layer of charcoal briquettes in a charcoal grill equipped with a rotating spit. Let the coals burn until white ash appears on the surface.

Thread the spareribs on the spit, running the spit through the meat over and under alternate pairs of ribs. Then secure them at both ends with the sliding prongs. Fit the spit into place about 6 inches above the surface of the coals and barbecue the ribs for 45 minutes, or until they are lightly and evenly browned. Watch carefully for any sign of burning and regulate the height of the spit accordingly.

With a pastry brush, spread the red sauce evenly on both sides of the spareribs. Basting the ribs every 5 minutes or so, continue to barbecue them for about 30 minutes longer, or until they are richly colored and glazed with sauce.

To serve, remove the spit from the grill, unscrew the prongs and slide the spareribs off the spit onto a heated platter. Before serving, insert skewers into each section of ribs if you like.

Red Pork Chili

To serve 4

1½ pounds lean boneless pork, trimmed of excess fat and cut into 1-inch cubes	3 tablespoons lard 2 cups fresh red chili sauce *(below)* 3 cups freshly cooked rice

Pat the pork cubes dry with paper towels. In a heavy 12-inch skillet, melt the lard over moderate heat until it is very hot but not smoking. Brown the pork in the hot fat, turning the cubes frequently with tongs and regulating the heat so that they color deeply and evenly without burning.

Stir in the red chili sauce and bring to a boil over high heat. Then reduce the heat to low and simmer partially covered for 35 to 40 minutes, or until the pork shows no resistance when pierced deeply with the point of a small sharp knife. Transfer the pork chili to a heated bowl and serve at once, accompanied by the rice.

Fresh Red Chili Sauce

To make 2 to 3 cups

	½ cup coarsely chopped onions
½ pound fresh hot red chilies, stemmed, seeded and coarsely chopped *(caution: see note, page 3)* 1 cup boiling water	¼ cup vegetable oil 2 tablespoons coarsely chopped garlic 2 teaspoons dried oregano 2 teaspoons salt

Combine the chilies and boiling water in a bowl and let them steep for about 10 minutes. Transfer the mixture to an electric blender and blend at high speed for 30 seconds. Turn off the machine, scrape down the sides of the jar with a rubber spatula, and add the onions, oil, garlic, oregano and salt. Blend until the chili sauce is reduced to a smooth purée, then taste for seasoning.

Fresh red chili sauce may be used as the base for red pork chili *(above)* or served as an accompaniment to tacos and enchiladas *(Recipe Index)*.

Texas Chili con Carne

To serve 6 to 8

6 dried *ancho* chilies, plus 8 dried hot red chilies, each about 2 inches long *(caution: see note, page 3)*
3½ cups boiling water
½ pound beef suet, preferably kidney suet, cut into ½-inch bits
3 pounds lean boneless venison or beef chuck, trimmed of excess fat, sliced ½ inch thick and cut into ½-inch cubes
3 medium-sized bay leaves, finely crumbled

1 tablespoon cumin seeds
2 tablespoons coarsely chopped garlic
4 teaspoons dried oregano
3 tablespoons paprika
1 tablespoon sugar
1 tablespoon salt
3 tablespoons yellow cornmeal
1 teaspoon ground hot red pepper (cayenne; optional)
Freshly cooked pinto beans *(page 40)*
9 cups freshly cooked rice made from 3 cups long-grain white rice

Under cold running water, pull the stems off the *ancho* and red chilies. Tear the chilies in half and brush out their seeds. With a small sharp knife, cut away any large ribs. Chop the chilies coarsely, drop them into a bowl, and pour the boiling water over them. Let them soak for at least 30 minutes, then strain the soaking liquid through a sieve set over a bowl and reserve it. Set the chilies aside.

In a heavy 5- to 6-quart casserole, cook the beef suet over moderate heat, stirring frequently until it has rendered all its fat. With a slotted spoon, remove and discard the suet bits. Pour off all but about ¼ cup of the fat remaining in the pot.

Add the venison or beef cubes to the casserole and, stirring constantly, cook over moderate heat until the pieces of meat are firm but not brown. Add 2½ cups of the reserved chili-soaking liquid and bring it to a boil over high heat. Drop in the bay leaves and reduce the heat to low. Simmer partially covered for 1 hour, stirring the mixture from time to time.

Meanwhile, place the cumin seeds in a small ungreased skillet and, sliding the pan back and forth frequently, toast the seeds over low heat for 10 minutes. Drop the seeds into the jar of an electric blender and blend at high speed for 30 seconds. Turn off the machine, add the *ancho* and red chilies, the remaining chili-soaking liquid, the garlic, oregano, paprika, sugar and salt, and blend again at high speed until all of the ingredients are reduced to a smooth purée.

When the meat has cooked its allotted time, stir in the chili purée. Simmer partially covered for 30 minutes. Then, stirring constantly, pour in the cornmeal in a slow stream and cook over high heat until the chili comes to a boil and thickens lightly. Taste the chili for seasoning and add the ground hot red pepper if desired.

Serve the chili con carne directly from the casserole, or from a heated tureen or serving bowl. Mound the pinto beans and the rice in separate bowls and present them with the chili.

Zuñi Green-Chili Stew

To serve 6 to 8

3 pounds boneless lamb shoulder, trimmed of excess fat and cut into 1½-inch cubes
3 tablespoons flour
¼ cup vegetable oil
1½ cups finely chopped onions
2 teaspoons finely chopped garlic
2 cups water
Two 1-pound 14-ounce cans hominy
6 small fresh hot green chilies, stemmed, seeded and finely chopped *(caution: see note, page 3)*

6 tablespoons finely chopped fresh parsley
6 whole juniper berries and 2 teaspoons dried oregano, pulverized with a mortar and pestle or wrapped in a kitchen towel and finely crushed with a kitchen mallet or the side of a heavy cleaver
2 teaspoons salt
¼ teaspoon freshly ground black pepper

Preheat the oven to 350°. Pat the cubes of lamb completely dry with paper towels. Then roll the meat in the flour to coat all sides evenly, and vigorously shake off the excess flour.

In a heavy 10- to 12-inch skillet, heat the oil over high heat until a light haze forms above it. Brown the lamb in the hot fat, seven or eight pieces at a time, turning the cubes frequently and regulating the heat so that they color deeply and evenly without burning. As they brown, transfer the lamb cubes to a heavy 6- to 8-quart baking-serving casserole.

Add the onions and garlic to the fat remaining in the skillet and, stirring frequently, cook over moderate heat for about 5 minutes, or until they are soft and translucent but not brown. Pour in the water and bring to a boil over high heat, meanwhile scraping in the brown particles that cling to the bottom and sides of the skillet. Pour the contents of the skillet over the lamb.

Stir in the hominy and its liquid, the chilies, 4 tablespoons of the parsley, the crushed juniper berries and oregano, and the salt and pepper. Bring to a boil over high heat, then cover tightly and cook in the middle of the oven for 1½ hours, or until the lamb is tender and shows no resistance when pierced deeply with the point of a small sharp knife. (The stew should be kept at a gentle simmer. Check the pot from time to time and regulate the oven heat as necessary.)

Taste the stew for seasoning, scatter the remaining 2 tablespoons of parsley on top and serve at once directly from the casserole.

Cowboy Short Ribs with Cornmeal Dumplings

To serve 6 to 8

SHORT-RIB STEW

2 small fresh or dried hot red chilies, each about 1½ inches long, stemmed, seeded and coarsely chopped (*caution: see note, page 3*)
1 tablespoon finely chopped garlic
½ teaspoon ground nutmeg
1 teaspoon freshly ground black pepper
2 teaspoons sugar
2 tablespoons soy sauce

4 pounds lean short ribs of beef, cut into 2-inch-long pieces
1½ teaspoons salt
1 cup flour
4 tablespoons lard
1 large onion, peeled and sliced crosswise into ¼-inch-thick rounds
5 medium-sized firm ripe tomatoes, stemmed, peeled and coarsely chopped
12 ounces (1½ cups) beer

With a mortar and pestle, or in a small bowl with the back of a spoon, crush the two red chilies, garlic, nutmeg and ½ teaspoon of the black pepper together. Add the sugar and soy sauce, and pound the mixture to a smooth paste. Set aside.

Pat the short ribs completely dry with paper towels and season them on all sides with 1½ teaspoons of salt and the remaining ½ teaspoon of black pepper. One at a time, roll the short ribs about in the flour to coat them evenly, then vigorously shake off the excess flour.

Melt the lard over moderate heat in a heavy 5- to 6-quart casserole at least 10 inches in diameter. Brown the short ribs in the hot fat, five or six pieces at a time, turning them frequently with tongs and regulating the heat so that they color richly and evenly on all sides without burning. As they brown, transfer the ribs to a plate.

Pour off all but about 2 tablespoons of the fat remaining in the casserole and add the onion slices. Stirring frequently, cook for about 5 minutes, until the onion slices are soft and translucent but not brown. Add the tomatoes and the reserved chili paste and cook briskly, stirring from time to time, until the mixture is thick enough to hold its shape almost solidly in a spoon.

Return the meat and the liquid that has accumulated around it to the casserole, stir in the beer and bring to a boil over high heat. Reduce the heat to its lowest setting, partially cover the pot and simmer for about 2 hours, or until the short ribs are tender and show no resistance when pierced with the point of a small sharp knife. Taste for seasoning.

DUMPLINGS
2 cups water
2 teaspoons salt
1 cup yellow cornmeal
2 tablespoons butter
¼ cup finely chopped onions
1 egg, lightly beaten
1 cup unsifted flour
2 teaspoons double-acting baking powder
⅛ teaspoon freshly ground black pepper
¾ cup freshly cooked, frozen or canned whole corn kernels, defrosted if frozen and thoroughly drained
½ teaspoon finely chopped fresh hot chilies, if desired

Meanwhile, prepare the dumplings in the following manner: In a small saucepan, bring the 2 cups of water and 2 teaspoons of salt to a boil over high heat. Stirring constantly, pour in the cornmeal in a slow, thin stream and cook briskly until the mixture is thick and smooth. Remove the pan from the heat and set it aside uncovered.

In a 6- to 8-inch skillet, melt the butter over moderate heat. When the foam subsides, add the chopped onions and, stirring frequently, cook for about 5 minutes, until they are soft but not brown. Scrape the entire contents of the skillet over the cornmeal and mix well, then stir in the egg.

Combine the cup of flour, the baking powder and ⅛ teaspoon black pepper, and sift them into the cornmeal mixture ½ cup at a time, beating well after each addition. Stir in the corn kernels and the ½ teaspoon of chopped chilies, if you are using them.

When the short ribs have cooked their allotted time, drop the dumpling mixture on top of the stew by the heaping tablespoon. Cover tightly and simmer undisturbed for 10 to 12 minutes longer. The dumplings are done when they are puffed and fluffy and a cake tester or toothpick inserted in the center of a dumpling comes out clean.

Serve at once, directly from the casserole. Or remove the dumplings, transfer the stew to a heated serving bowl and arrange the dumplings attractively on top.

Charcoal-broiled T-Bone or Porterhouse Steak

To serve 4 to 6

A 3½- to 4-pound T-bone or
  porterhouse steak, cut 2 inches

thick
Salt
Freshly ground black pepper

Light a 1- to 2-inch-thick layer of briquettes in a charcoal grill and let the coals burn until white ash appears on the surface.

Broil the steak about 4 inches from the heat until it is done to suit your taste, turning it once with heavy tongs or with a kitchen fork inserted into the outer rim of fat. Broil it about 7 to 8 minutes on each side for rare steak, 9 to 10 minutes for medium, and 11 to 12 minutes on each side for well done.

Transfer the steak to a heated platter, season it lightly with salt and a few grindings of pepper, and serve at once.

Olive Beef Stew (Typed on recipe card 3/28/74)

To serve 6 to 8

3 pounds lean beef chuck, trimmed
  of excess fat and cut into
  1½-inch cubes
2 teaspoons salt
1 teaspoon freshly ground black
  pepper
1 cup flour

½ cup olive oil
2 large onions, peeled and sliced
  crosswise into ¼-inch-thick
  rounds
1 tablespoon finely chopped garlic
1 cup dry vermouth
2 cups water
2 dozen large green olives

Preheat the oven to 350°. Pat the cubes of beef dry with paper towels and season them with the salt and pepper. Roll the cubes in the flour to coat all sides evenly, then vigorously shake off the excess flour.

In a heavy 4- or 5-quart casserole, heat the olive oil over moderate heat until a light haze forms above it. Brown the beef in the hot oil, 5 or 6 cubes at a time, turning them frequently with tongs and regulating the heat so that they color deeply and evenly without burning. As they brown, transfer the cubes to a plate. Add the onions and garlic to the fat remaining in the casserole and, stirring frequently, cook them for about 5 minutes, until they are soft and translucent but not brown. Pour in the vermouth and water and bring to a boil over high heat, meanwhile scraping in the brown particles that cling to the bottom and sides of the pot.

Stir in the beef and the liquid that has accumulated around it, cover

78

the casserole tightly, and braise in the middle of the oven for about 2 hours, or until the beef shows no resistance when pierced deeply with the point of a small sharp knife. (Check the beef from time to time and regulate the oven heat as necessary to keep the liquid at a gentle simmer.)

Meanwhile, drop the olives into enough boiling water to cover them completely and cook briskly for 2 or 3 minutes. Drain the olives in a sieve or colander and, with a small sharp knife, cut them from their pits in spiral strips. Discard the pits.

When the beef has cooked its allotted time, gently stir in the olives and simmer the stew over low heat for a few minutes to heat them through. Taste for seasoning and serve at once, directly from the casserole or from a heated bowl.

Rabbit in Tarragon Cream Gravy

To serve 4 to 6

A 3- to 3½-pound rabbit, thoroughly defrosted if frozen, cut into 12 serving pieces
1 teaspoon salt
¼ teaspoon ground white pepper

¾ cup flour
½ cup vegetable oil
1¾ cups chicken stock, fresh or canned
1 cup heavy cream
1 teaspoon crumbled dried tarragon

Pat the pieces of rabbit dry with paper towels and season them on all sides with the salt and white pepper. Roll the pieces in ½ cup of the flour to coat them evenly, and vigorously shake off the excess flour.

In a heavy 6- to 8-quart casserole, heat the oil over high heat until a light haze forms above it. Brown four or five pieces of rabbit at a time, starting them skin side down and turning them frequently with tongs. Regulate the heat so that the meat colors richly and evenly on all sides. As the pieces of rabbit brown, transfer them to a plate.

Pour off all but about 4 tablespoons of the fat remaining in the casserole, then add the remaining ¼ cup of flour and mix well. Stirring constantly with a wire whisk, pour in the chicken stock in a slow, thin stream and cook over high heat until the sauce comes to a boil, thickens and is smooth. Whisk in the cream and tarragon and return the rabbit and the juices that have accumulated around it to the casserole. Reduce the heat to low, cover tightly and simmer for about 1 hour, or until the rabbit is tender but not falling apart.

Taste for seasoning and serve the rabbit at once, directly from the casserole. Or, if you prefer, arrange the pieces of rabbit in a deep heated platter and ladle the tarragon cream gravy over them.

BREADS

Date, Pecan and Orange Bread
To make one 9-by-5-by-3-inch loaf

5 tablespoons butter, softened
4 tablespoons plus 2 cups unsifted flour
8 ounces pitted dates, cut into small bits with kitchen scissors (about 1 cup)
½ cup finely chopped pecans
4 teaspoons finely chopped fresh orange peel
1 teaspoon double-acting baking powder
1 teaspoon baking soda
1 teaspoon salt
1 cup sugar
1 egg
1 cup strained fresh orange juice

Preheat the oven to 350°. With a pastry brush, spread 1 tablespoon of the softened butter over the bottom and sides of a 9-by-5-by-3-inch loaf pan. Add 2 tablespoons of the flour and tip the pan from side to side to distribute it evenly. Invert the pan and rap it sharply to remove excess flour.

Place the dates, pecans and orange peel in a bowl, add 2 tablespoons of flour, and toss together gently but thoroughly. Combine the remaining 2 cups of flour, the baking powder, soda and salt, and sift them together into a bowl. Set aside.

In a deep bowl, cream the remaining 4 tablespoons of butter and the sugar by beating and mashing them against the sides of the bowl with the back of a large spoon until the mixture is light and fluffy. Beat in the egg. Add about ½ cup of the flour mixture and, when it is incorporated, beat in ¼ cup of the orange juice. Repeat three times, alternating ½ cup of the flour with ¼ cup of orange juice and beating well after each addition. Stir in the reserved floured fruit and nuts.

Pour the batter into the prepared pan and bake in the middle of the oven for 50 to 60 minutes, or until a toothpick or cake tester inserted in the center comes out clean. Let the bread cool in the pan for 4 or 5 minutes, then turn it out on a wire rack to cool completely to room temperature before serving.

Wheat-Germ Hamburger Buns

To make about 1½ dozen 4-inch
round buns

4 teaspoons salt

2 cups lukewarm water (110° to
  115°)

2 eggs

2 packages active dry yeast

8 tablespoons butter, cut into
  ½-inch bits and softened, plus

2 teaspoons plus ¼ cup sugar

2 tablespoons butter, softened

5 to 6 cups unsifted flour

1 egg lightly beaten with

1 cup wheat germ

  1 tablespoon milk

⅔ cup dry milk solids

3 tablespoons sesame seeds

Pour ½ cup of the lukewarm water into a small bowl and sprinkle the yeast and 2 teaspoons of the sugar over it. Let the yeast and sugar rest for 2 or 3 minutes, then mix well. Set in a warm, draft-free place (such as an unlighted oven) for about 10 minutes, or until the yeast bubbles up and the mixture almost doubles in volume.

Place 5 cups of the flour, the remaining ¼ cup of sugar, the wheat germ, dry milk solids and salt in a deep mixing bowl and make a well in the center. Add the yeast mixture, the remaining 1½ cups of lukewarm water, the eggs and the 8 tablespoons of butter bits and, with a large spoon, gradually incorporate the dry ingredients into the liquid ones. Stir until the mixture can be gathered into a medium-soft ball.

Transfer the ball to a lightly floured surface and knead, pushing the dough down with the heels of your hands, pressing it forward and folding it back on itself. Incorporate up to 1 cup more flour by the tablespoonful as you knead, adding only enough to make a nonsticky dough. Continue kneading for 10 minutes, until the dough is smooth and elastic.

With a pastry brush, spread 1 tablespoon of the softened butter inside a large bowl. Place the dough in the bowl and turn the ball to butter the entire surface. Drape the bowl with a kitchen towel and set it in the draft-free place for 1½ hours, or until the dough doubles in volume.

Brush the remaining tablespoon of softened butter evenly over two large baking sheets. Punch the dough down with a blow of your fist, set it on a lightly floured surface and, with your hands, roll it into a cylinder about 18 inches long and 4 inches in diameter. Cut the cylinder into 1-inch-thick rounds and shape each round into a bun about 3 inches in diameter and 1½ inches thick. Arrange the buns 1½ inches apart on the buttered baking sheets and drape them with towels. Set the buns in the draft-free place to rise for about 45 minutes, or until doubled in volume.

Preheat the oven to 400°. Brush the buns with the egg-and-milk mixture and sprinkle each one with ½ teaspoon of the sesame seeds. Bake in the middle of the oven for 15 minutes, or until the hamburger buns are golden brown. Slide the buns onto wire racks to cool before serving.

Mormon Rye Bread

To make one 9-by-5-by-3-inch loaf

1 cup lukewarm water (110° to
    115°)
1 package active dry yeast
1 teaspoon granulated sugar
1 cup rye flour
2½ to 3 cups unsifted all-purpose
    flour

¼ cup dark brown sugar
1 teaspoon salt
¼ cup honey
½ cup vegetable shortening, cut
    into ½-inch bits and softened
2 tablespoons butter, softened
1 egg, beaten lightly with
    1 tablespoon milk

Pour ¼ cup of the lukewarm water into a small bowl and sprinkle the yeast and granulated sugar over it. Let the yeast and sugar rest for 2 or 3 minutes, then mix well. Set in a warm, draft-free place (such as an unlighted oven) for about 10 minutes, or until the yeast bubbles up and the mixture almost doubles in volume.

Place the rye flour, 2 cups of all-purpose flour, the brown sugar and salt in a deep mixing bowl and make a well in the center. Add the yeast mixture, the remaining ¾ cup of lukewarm water, the honey and vegetable-shortening bits. With a large spoon, gradually incorporate the dry ingredients into the liquid ones and continue to stir until the mixture is smooth and can be gathered into a medium-soft ball. If the dough becomes too stiff to stir easily, mix it with your hands.

Transfer the ball to a lightly floured surface and knead, pushing the dough down with the heels of your hands, pressing it forward and folding it back on itself. Incorporate up to 1 cup more all-purpose flour by the tablespoonful as you knead, adding only enough to make a smooth dough that is no longer sticky. Then continue kneading for about 10 minutes, until the dough is smooth and elastic.

With a pastry brush, spread 1 tablespoon of the softened butter evenly inside a large bowl. Place the dough in the bowl and turn the ball about to butter the entire surface. Drape the bowl with a kitchen towel and set it aside in the warm, draft-free place for approximately 1½ hours, or until the dough doubles in volume.

Brush the remaining tablespoon of softened butter over the bottom and sides of a 9-by-5-by-3-inch loaf pan. Punch the dough down with a blow of your fist and, on a lightly floured surface, shape the dough into a loaf about 8 inches long and 4 inches wide. Place the loaf in the buttered pan and set it in the warm, draft-free place for about 45 minutes, or until it has doubled in volume.

Preheat the oven to 375°. (If you have used the oven to let the loaf rise, gently transfer it to another warm place to rest while the oven heats.) Brush the loaf with the egg-and-milk mixture and bake in the middle of the oven for 30 to 35 minutes, or until the top is golden brown. To test for doneness, turn the loaf out and rap the bottom sharply with your knuckles. The loaf should sound hollow; if not, return it to the pan and bake for 5 to 10 minutes longer. Place the Mormon rye bread on a wire rack and cool completely to room temperature before serving.

Navajo Fry Bread

To make three 8-inch round breads

2 cups unsifted flour
½ cup dry milk solids
2 teaspoons double-acting baking
  powder

½ teaspoon salt
2 tablespoons lard, cut into ½-inch
  bits, plus 1 pound lard for deep
  frying
½ cup ice water

Combine the flour, dry milk solids, baking powder and salt, and sift them into a deep bowl. Add the 2 tablespoons of lard bits and, with your fingertips, rub the flour and fat together until the mixture resembles flakes of coarse meal. Pour in the water and toss the ingredients together until the dough can be gathered into a ball. Drape the bowl with a kitchen towel and let the dough rest at room temperature for about 2 hours.

After the resting period, cut the dough into three equal pieces. Then, on a lightly floured surface, roll each piece into a rough circle about 8 inches in diameter and ¼ inch thick. With a small sharp knife, cut two 4- to 5-inch-long parallel slits completely through the dough down the center of each round, spacing the slits about 1 inch apart.

In a heavy 10-inch skillet, melt the remaining pound of lard over moderate heat until it is very hot but not smoking. The melted fat should be about 1 inch deep; add more lard if necessary. Fry the breads one at a time for about 2 minutes on each side, turning them once with tongs or a slotted spatula. The bread will puff slightly and become crisp and brown. Drain the Navajo fry bread on paper towels and serve warm.

Monkey Bread

To make two 9-inch ring loaves

2 cups water
2 medium-sized boiling potatoes, peeled and quartered
1 package active dry yeast
1 teaspoon plus ½ cup sugar
5½ to 6½ cups unsifted flour
2 teaspoons salt

2 eggs, lightly beaten
1 cup lukewarm milk (110° to 115°)
½ cup vegetable shortening
1 tablespoon butter, softened, plus ½ pound butter, melted and cooled

Reportedly this bread was named by movie star ZaSu Pitts, who explained that it was the kind of loaf "you had to monkey around with."

Bring the water to a boil in a small heavy saucepan. Drop in the potatoes and boil briskly, uncovered, until a piece of potato can be easily mashed against the side of the pan with the back of a fork. Drain the potatoes in a sieve set over a bowl and pat them dry with paper towels. (Measure and reserve ¼ cup of the potato water.) Purée the potatoes through a food mill set over a bowl, or mash them with the back of a fork. You should have about 1 cup of purée.

When the reserved potato water has cooled to lukewarm (110° to 115°), pour it into a shallow bowl. Add the yeast and 1 teaspoon of the sugar and let the mixture rest for 2 to 3 minutes, then stir well. Set the bowl in a warm, draft-free place (such as an unlighted oven) for 5 minutes, or until the yeast bubbles and the mixture almost doubles in volume.

Combine 5½ cups of the flour, the remaining ½ cup of sugar and the salt in a deep mixing bowl and make a well in the center. Add the potato purée, the yeast mixture and the eggs, milk and vegetable shortening. With a large spoon, mix the ingredients together and stir until the dough is smooth and can be gathered into a soft ball.

Place the ball on a lightly floured surface and knead, pushing the dough down with the heels of your hands, pressing it forward and folding it back on itself. As you knead, sprinkle flour over the ball by the tablespoonful, adding up to 1 cup of flour if necessary to make a firm dough. Continue to knead for about 10 minutes, or until the dough is smooth, shiny and elastic.

With a pastry brush, spread the tablespoon of softened butter evenly inside a deep mixing bowl. Place the ball in the bowl and turn it around to butter the entire surface of the dough. Drape the bowl loosely with a kitchen towel and put it in the draft-free place for about 1½ hours, until the dough doubles in volume.

With a pastry brush, spread 2 tablespoons of the melted butter evenly over the bottom and sides of two 9-inch tube pans. Punch the dough down with a blow of your fist and place it on a lightly floured surface. With your hands, pat and shape the dough into a rectangle 14 inches long, 12 inches wide and about ½ inch thick. Using a ruler and a pastry wheel or sharp knife, cut the rectangle into diamonds about 2 inches long and 2 inches wide.

To assemble the monkey bread, immerse one diamond at a time in the remaining melted butter and arrange a layer of diamonds side by side in a ring on the bottom of each buttered tube pan. Repeat with two more layers of butter-coated diamonds, arranging each successive layer so that it fits over the spaces left in the previous ring. (Do not worry that the diamonds do not fill all the available space; as they rise and bake they will expand.) Drape the pans loosely with towels and set them aside in the draft-free place for about 1 hour, or until the loaves double in volume.

Preheat the oven to 375°. (If you have used the oven to let the loaves rise, gently transfer the pans to another warm place to rest while the oven heats.) Bake the monkey bread in the middle of the oven for 30 to 35 minutes, or until the loaves are golden brown. To test for doneness, turn the loaves out and rap the bottoms sharply with your knuckles. The loaves should sound hollow; if they do not, return them to their pans and bake for 5 to 10 minutes longer.

Turn the bread out on wire racks and let it cool before serving. Monkey bread is never sliced. Instead each diner pulls a diamond-shaped piece from the loaf.

Cowboy Soda Biscuits

To make about 15 biscuits

2¼ cups unsifted flour
1 teaspoon baking soda
1 teaspoon salt

3 tablespoons lard, cut into ½-inch bits, plus ½ pound lard for deep frying
1 cup buttermilk or sour milk

Combine the flour, baking soda and salt in a deep bowl. Add the 3 table-spoons of lard bits and, with your fingertips, rub the flour and fat together until they resemble flakes of coarse meal. Pour in the buttermilk or sour milk and beat vigorously with a spoon to make a smooth dough.

Over moderate heat, melt the remaining ½ pound of lard in a Dutch oven or heavy casserole about 8 inches in diameter and 4 or 5 inches deep. Heat the fat until it is very hot but not smoking.

To shape each biscuit, cut off about 2 tablespoons of the dough and, flouring your hands lightly as you proceed, pat the dough into a ball about 1½ inches in diameter. Drop two or three biscuits at a time into the

Continued on next page

hot fat, turning them about with a slotted spoon to coat them on all sides with the fat. When all the biscuits have been added to the pot, cover it tightly and fry the biscuits over moderate heat for 4 minutes. Turn the biscuits over with a slotted spoon, cover again and fry for 4 minutes longer, or until they are evenly browned and puffed. Transfer the biscuits to paper towels to drain briefly, and serve them hot.

Mormon Johnnycake

To make one 9-by-9-inch cake

1 tablespoon butter, softened, plus 2 tablespoons butter, melted and cooled	2 tablespoons honey
	½ cup unsifted flour
	1 teaspoon baking soda
2 eggs	1 teaspoon salt
2 cups buttermilk	2 cups yellow cornmeal

Preheat the oven to 425°. With a pastry brush, spread the tablespoon of softened butter evenly over the bottom and sides of a 9-by-9-by-2-inch baking dish. Set the dish aside.

In a deep mixing bowl, beat the eggs to a froth with a wire whisk. Beat in the buttermilk and honey, then add the flour, baking soda and salt. When the batter is smooth, beat in the cornmeal about ½ cup at a time. Stir in the 2 tablespoons of cooled melted butter and pour the batter into the buttered dish, spreading it evenly and smoothing the top with a rubber spatula.

Bake the johnnycake in the middle of the oven for about 20 minutes, or until the cake begins to pull away from the sides of the dish and the top is golden brown and crusty. Serve the Mormon johnnycake at once, directly from the baking dish.

DESSERTS & PASTRIES

Glazed Oranges

To serve 6

6 navel or Temple oranges
1 cup dry white wine
2 tablespoons red wine vinegar
¾ cup sugar

A 2-inch cinnamon stick and 10
    whole cloves, wrapped together
    in cheesecloth
2 tablespoons Grand Marnier or
    other orange liqueur (optional)

With a small sharp knife, remove the skin from two of the oranges without cutting into the bitter white pith beneath it. Cut the peel into strips about ⅛ inch wide, drop them into enough boiling water to cover them completely and cook briskly for about 2 minutes. With a slotted spoon, transfer the strips to paper towels to drain.

Cut the white outer pith and membrane from the two skinned oranges, using short sawing motions. Then cut away and discard the peel, pith and all the white outside membrane from the remaining four oranges.

Combine the wine, vinegar, sugar, and the cheesecloth-wrapped cinnamon and cloves in a 3- to 4-quart enameled or stainless-steel saucepan and bring to a boil over high heat, stirring until the sugar dissolves. Add the oranges and the strips of orange peel, and turn them about with a spoon to coat them evenly with the syrup. Reduce the heat to low, then simmer uncovered for 15 minutes, turning the oranges over frequently.

With a slotted spoon, transfer the oranges and peel to a deep bowl. Pick out and discard the cheesecloth bag of spices and taste the syrup for sweetness. If you like, you may add 1 or 2 tablespoons of orange liqueur to the syrup. Pour the syrup over the oranges and cool to room temperature. Cover the bowl tightly with foil or plastic wrap and refrigerate the oranges for at least 2 hours to chill them thoroughly before serving.

Lalla Rookh
RUM ICE CREAM

To make about 2 quarts

4 cups heavy cream
¾ cup sugar

A 1½-inch piece of vanilla bean
⅛ teaspoon salt
¾ cup dark rum

This ice cream received its fanciful title near the turn of the century, when it was considered stylish to give desserts glamorous names. (The original recipe appeared in The Guild Cook Book, compiled by the ladies of St. Paul's Episcopal Church, Waco, Texas, in 1888.) Its inspiration was Lalla Rookh, a book of Oriental tales in verse written by the Irish poet Thomas Moore.

Combine 1 cup of the cream with the sugar, vanilla bean and salt in a small heavy saucepan and place the pan over low heat. Stir until the sugar dissolves, then simmer undisturbed until small bubbles appear around the edges of the pan. Remove the pan from the heat and pick out the vanilla bean. Split the bean in half lengthwise and, with the tip of a small sharp knife, scrape the vanilla seeds into the cream mixture. When the mixture has cooled to room temperature, stir in the remaining 3 cups of cream and the rum.

Pack a 2-quart ice-cream freezer with layers of finely crushed or cracked ice and coarse rock salt in the proportions recommended by the freezer manufacturer. Add cold water if the manufacturer advises it. Then ladle the cream mixture into the ice-cream can and cover it.

If you have a hand ice-cream maker, fill it and let it stand for 3 or 4 minutes before beginning to turn the handle. It may take 15 minutes or more of turning for the ice cream to freeze, but do not stop turning at any time or the ice cream may be lumpy. When the handle can barely be moved, the ice cream is ready to serve. If you wish to keep it for an hour or two before serving it, remove the lid and dasher. Scrape the ice cream off the dasher and pack all the ice cream firmly in the can with a spoon. Cover the can securely, pour off any water in the bucket and repack the ice and salt solidly around the can.

If you have an electric ice-cream maker, fill and cover the can, turn it on and let it churn for about 15 minutes, or until the motor slows or actually stops. Serve the ice cream immediately or follow the procedure above to keep it for an hour or two.

Lacking an ice-cream maker, pour the ice cream into three or four ice-cube trays from which the dividers have been removed, spreading it evenly and smoothing the top with a spatula. Freeze for 3 to 4 hours, stirring every 30 minutes or so and scraping into it the ice particles that form around the edges of the trays.

Tightly covered, the ice cream may safely be kept in the freezer for several weeks. Before serving, place it in the refrigerator for 20 or 30 minutes to let it soften slightly so that it can easily be served.

San Antonio Fruit Ice Cream
To make about 1½ quarts

1¼ cups strained fresh grapefruit juice
¾ cup strained fresh orange juice
3 tablespoons strained fresh lemon juice
½ to 1 cup sugar
A 1-pound 4-ounce can mangoes, drained and coarsely chopped (about 2½ cups)

An 8½- to 9-ounce can pears, drained and coarsely chopped (about 1¼ cups)
½ cup drained canned pineapple chunks
2 large ripe bananas, peeled and cut in chunks
1 cup heavy cream
3 egg whites

Pour the grapefruit, orange and lemon juice into a large mixing bowl, add ½ cup of sugar, and stir until it dissolves. Stir in the mangoes, pears, pineapple and bananas. Ladle 2 or 3 cups of the mixture into the jar of an electric blender and blend at high speed for 10 seconds. Turn off the machine, scrape down the sides of the jar with a rubber spatula, and blend again until the fruit is reduced to a purée. Scrape the purée into a bowl and blend the remaining fruit mixture in the same fashion.

Stir the heavy cream into the purée, taste and add up to ½ cup more sugar by the tablespoonful if desired. Then pour the mixture into three ice-cube trays from which the dividers have been removed, dividing it evenly among them. Freeze for about 2 hours, or until the ice cream is slushy, stirring it every 30 minutes or so and scraping into it the ice particles that form around the edges of the trays.

In a deep bowl, beat the egg whites with a wire whisk or a rotary or electric beater until they are stiff enough to stand in unwavering peaks on the whisk or beater when it is lifted from the bowl. Working quickly, scrape the ice-cream mixture from the trays into a bowl with a rubber spatula. Scoop the egg whites over the ice cream and mix them together gently but thoroughly with a large spoon or table fork. Return the mixture to the trays, spreading it evenly and smoothing the tops with the spatula. Freeze for 2 or 3 hours longer, or until the ice cream is firm.

Short-Crust Pastry

To make one 9-inch pie shell

6 tablespoons unsalted butter,
   chilled and cut into ¼-inch bits,
   plus 1 tablespoon butter, softened
2 tablespoons lard, chilled and cut

into ¼-inch bits
1½ cups all-purpose flour
1 tablespoon sugar
¼ teaspoon salt
3 to 4 tablespoons ice water

PASTRY DOUGH: In a large chilled bowl, combine the butter bits, lard, flour, sugar and salt. With your fingertips rub the flour and fat together until they look like flakes of coarse meal. Do not let the mixture become oily. Pour 3 tablespoons of ice water over the mixture all at once, toss together lightly and gather the dough into a ball. If the dough crumbles, add up to 1 tablespoon more ice water, drop by drop, until the particles adhere. Dust the pastry dough with a little flour and wrap it in wax paper. Refrigerate for at least 1 hour before using.

TO MAKE AN UNFILLED PIE SHELL: Spread 1 tablespoon of softened butter over the bottom and sides of a 9-inch pie pan with a pastry brush.

On a lightly floured surface, pat the chilled short-crust pastry dough into a rough circle about 1 inch thick. Dust a little flour over and under it, and roll it out from the center to within an inch of the far edge of the circle. Lift the dough and turn it clockwise about 2 inches; roll again from the center to within an inch or so of the far edge. Repeat—lifting, turning, rolling—until the circle is about ⅛ inch thick and 13 to 14 inches in diameter. If the dough sticks to the board or table, lift it gently with a metal spatula and sprinkle a little flour under it.

Drape the dough over the rolling pin, lift it up, and unroll it slackly over the buttered pie pan. Gently press the dough into the bottom and sides of the pan, taking care not to stretch it. With a pair of scissors, cut off the excess dough from the edges, leaving a 1-inch overhang all around the outside rim.

TO MAKE A PARTIALLY BAKED PIE SHELL: Preheat the oven to 400°. Roll out the short-crust pastry dough as described above and fit it into a buttered 9-inch pie pan. To prevent the unfilled pie shell from buckling as it bakes, spread a sheet of buttered aluminum foil across the pan and press it gently into the bottom and against the sides of the pie shell. Bake in the middle of the oven for 10 minutes, then remove the foil. Bake for another 2 or 3 minutes, or until the pastry is delicately browned. Remove the pie shell from the oven and cool to room temperature before filling.

Osgood Pie

To make one 9-inch pie

4 egg whites
4 egg yolks
1 cup sugar
1 tablespoon flour
1 teaspoon ground cinnamon
½ teaspoon ground cloves
½ teaspoon ground nutmeg
3 tablespoons distilled white
vinegar
2 tablespoons bourbon or dry sherry
1 tablespoon butter, melted and
cooled
1 cup finely chopped pecans
1 cup seedless raisins
A 9-inch short-crust pastry shell
partially baked and cooled
(opposite)

Preheat the oven to 350°. With a wire whisk or a rotary or electric beater, beat the egg whites until they are stiff enough to stand in unwavering peaks on the whisk or beater when it is lifted from the bowl.

In a separate bowl but with the same beater unwashed, beat the egg yolks to a froth. Combine the sugar, flour, cinnamon, cloves and nutmeg in a sifter and sprinkle them over the yolks about ½ cup at a time, beating well after each addition. Beat in the vinegar, bourbon or sherry, and cooled melted butter and, when they are thoroughly incorporated, stir in the pecans and raisins.

With a rubber spatula, scoop the egg whites over the egg-yolk mixture and fold them together gently until no trace of white remains. Pour the filling mixture into the pie shell and smooth the top with the spatula. Bake in the middle of the oven for 25 to 30 minutes, or until the top is puffed and delicately browned and the filling remains firm when the pie is shaken gently.

Cool the Osgood pie to room temperature before serving.

Lime Chiffon Pie

To make one 9-inch pie

CRUST

1⅓ cups crumbs made from graham crackers pulverized in a blender or wrapped in a towel	and finely crushed with a rolling pin 4 tablespoons butter, melted

Preheat the oven to 375°. First prepare the crust in the following manner: Combine the graham-cracker crumbs and melted butter in a 9-inch pie pan and stir until all the crumbs are moistened. Spread the crumb mixture in the bottom of the pan. Place another 9-inch pie pan over the crumbs and press it down firmly to spread the crust mixture evenly across the bottom and along the sides of the first pan. Remove the second pan and smooth the top edges of the crust with your fingers. Bake in the middle of the oven for 8 to 10 minutes, or until the crust is delicately colored. Set it aside to cool to room temperature.

FILLING

¼ cup water	1 teaspoon finely grated fresh lime peel
1 envelope unflavored gelatin	
¾ cup plus ½ cup sugar	4 egg whites
¾ cup strained fresh lime juice	4 egg yolks

Meanwhile, prepare the filling. Pour the water into a small bowl, pour in the gelatin and let it soften for 2 or 3 minutes. Combine ¾ cup of the sugar, the lime juice and lime peel in a small pan and bring to a boil over high heat, stirring until the sugar dissolves. Reduce the heat to low, pour in the gelatin mixture and continue to stir until the gelatin is dissolved. Remove the pan from the heat.

With a wire whisk or a rotary or electric beater, beat the egg whites until they are thick enough to form soft peaks on the whisk or beater when it is lifted from the bowl. Add the remaining ½ cup of sugar and continue to beat until the egg whites are stiff.

In a separate bowl but with the same beater unwashed, beat the egg yolks for 1 or 2 minutes. Beating constantly, pour in the lime gelatin in a slow, thin stream, and continue to beat until the mixture is smooth. Set the bowl into another large bowl half filled with crushed ice or ice cubes and water and stir with a spoon until the mixture is quite cold and begins to thicken. Beat thoroughly with a wire whisk or rotary beater to be sure the mixture is perfectly smooth.

With a rubber spatula, scoop the beaten egg whites over the egg-yolk-and-gelatin mixture and fold them together gently but thoroughly. Then pour the filling into the cooled crust, spreading it evenly and smoothing the top with the spatula. Drape wax paper over the top and refrigerate the pie for about 3 hours, until firm to the touch. Serve the pie chilled.

Pecan Cake

To make one 10-inch cake ring

2½ cups seedless raisins
¾ to 1¼ cups bourbon
13 tablespoons butter, softened
2 tablespoons plus 3 cups unsifted
flour
1½ teaspoons double-acting
baking powder
1½ teaspoons ground nutmeg
1 teaspoon salt
1½ cups sugar
5 eggs
3 cups coarsely chopped pecans
(about 12 ounces)

Mix the raisins and ¾ cup of bourbon together in a bowl and let them steep for at least 30 minutes, stirring from time to time.

Preheat the oven to 325°. With a pastry brush, spread 1 tablespoon of softened butter over the bottom and sides of a 10-inch tube cake pan. Add 2 tablespoons of the flour and tip the pan from side to side to distribute it evenly. Invert the pan and rap the bottom sharply to remove the excess flour. Set the pan aside.

Combine 2½ cups of the remaining flour with the baking powder, nutmeg and salt, and sift them together into a bowl.

In a deep mixing bowl, cream the remaining 12 tablespoons of softened butter and the sugar by beating and mashing them against the sides of the bowl with the back of a spoon until the mixture is light and fluffy. Beat in the eggs, one at a time, then add the flour-nutmeg mixture by the cupful, beating the batter well after each addition.

With a slotted spoon, transfer the raisins to a small bowl and pour the ¾ cup of bourbon into the batter. Mix well. Add the pecans and the remaining ½ cup of flour to the raisins and toss them together thoroughly. Then stir the raisin-and-nut mixture into the batter.

Pour the batter into the prepared pan, filling it about three quarters full and smoothing the top with a rubber spatula. Bake in the middle of the oven for about 1 hour and 10 minutes, or until a toothpick or cake tester inserted in the center comes out clean.

Let the cake cool in the pan for about 10 minutes, then turn it out on a wire rack to cool completely. Serve at once or, if you prefer, soak a double-thick 16-inch square of cheesecloth in ½ cup of additional bourbon and wrap the cloth around the cake. Cover it tightly with foil or plastic wrap and let it stand at room temperature for at least 48 hours before serving.

Grapefruit Cake with Cream-Cheese Icing

To make a 2-layer 9-inch cake

CAKE
2 tablespoons butter, softened
2 tablespoons all-purpose flour
2 cups cake flour (not the self-rising variety), sifted before measuring
2 teaspoons double-acting baking powder
½ teaspoon salt
⅓ cup strained fresh grapefruit

juice
⅓ cup vegetable oil
¼ cup water
4 egg whites
⅛ teaspoon cream of tartar
4 egg yolks
1 cup granulated sugar
1 tablespoon finely grated fresh grapefruit peel

Preheat the oven to 350°. With a pastry brush, spread the softened butter over the bottom and sides of two 9-inch layer-cake pans. Add 1 tablespoon of all-purpose flour to each pan and tip it from side to side to distribute the flour evenly. Invert the pans and rap them sharply to remove the excess flour.

Combine the cake flour, baking powder and salt, and sift them together into a bowl. Pour the grapefruit juice, vegetable oil and water into a glass measuring cup. Set aside.

With a wire whisk or a rotary or electric beater, beat the egg whites and cream of tartar until the whites are stiff enough to stand in unwavering peaks on the beater when it is lifted from the bowl. Set aside.

In a separate bowl but with the same beater, beat the egg yolks and granulated sugar together for 4 to 5 minutes, or until the mixture is thick. Beat in about ½ cup of the flour mixture and, when it is thoroughly incorporated, add about ¼ cup of the juice-and-oil mixture. Repeat three times, alternating ½ cup of the flour with ¼ cup of the juice and oil and beating the batter well after each addition. Stir in 1 tablespoon of grated grapefruit peel.

With a rubber spatula scoop the egg whites over the batter and fold them together gently but thoroughly. Pour the batter into the prepared pans, dividing it evenly between them and smoothing the tops with the spatula. Bake the cakes in the middle of the oven for about 25 minutes, or until a toothpick or cake tester inserted in the centers comes out clean. Let the cakes cool in the pans for 4 or 5 minutes, then turn them out onto wire racks to cool to room temperature.

ICING

1 large firm grapefruit	1 cup confectioners' sugar
2 eight-ounce packages cream cheese, cut into ½-inch bits and softened	2 tablespoons finely grated fresh grapefruit peel
	½ teaspoon vanilla extract

Meanwhile, prepare the cream-cheese icing in the following fashion: Wash the grapefruit and pat it dry with paper towels. With a small sharp knife, remove the skin without cutting into the bitter white pith beneath it. Cut the peel into strips about ⅛ inch wide and set them aside.

To section the grapefruit, cut the white outer pith and membrane away, using short sawing motions. Then cut along both sides of each membrane division to the core of the grapefruit. As each section is freed, carefully lift it out and set it aside on paper towels to drain.

In a deep bowl, cream the cream cheese and confectioners' sugar together by beating and mashing them against the sides of the bowl with the back of a large spoon until the mixture is light and fluffy. Beat in the grated grapefruit peel and vanilla extract.

When the cake is cool, place one layer upside down on an inverted cake pan. With a metal spatula, spread about ½ cup of the cream-cheese icing over this layer and put the top layer in place. Reserve ½ cup of the icing to make roses, as shown in the photographs on pages 96 and 97. Then spread the remaining icing evenly over the top and sides of the cake and decorate the sides with the reserved strips of grapefruit peel. Arrange the grapefruit sections and icing roses attractively on top and refrigerate the cake until ready to serve.

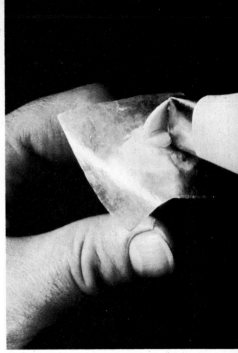

1 For each rose, squeeze a dot of icing onto the head of a No. 2 flower nail. Press a 1½-inch square of wax paper over the dot; the icing will hold it.

2 Hold the broad end of the tip of a No. 125 rose tube at the center of the nail. Rotate the nail clockwise and squeeze out enough icing to form a small cone.

How to Make an Icing Rose

With the correct equipment, and some practice, you can decorate a grapefruit cake *(recipe, page 94)* with icing roses as shapely as any that ever came from a professional baker. Notice that an icing rose is not made directly on the cake but on the flat head of a hand-held device shaped like a thumbtack and technically called a flower nail; the one shown in these pictures is a No. 2 nail. To form each part of the rose, you must squeeze the icing onto the flower nail through a pastry bag fitted with a No. 125 decorative rose tube. Both nail and tube can be bought at a specialty cookware shop *(or see the Shopping Guide, page 150)*. The bag, a cone made of paper, plastic or cloth, is open at both ends; the tube, which slips into the bag, is a smaller metal cone ending in a tapered slot. Follow the photographs step by step, using ½ cup of the cream-cheese icing—or, for practice, substitute ½ cup of vegetable shortening. Refrigerate each rose individually on the wax paper on which it was shaped. When you are ready to decorate the cake, transfer the roses from the paper by slipping the point of a knife carefully under each one.

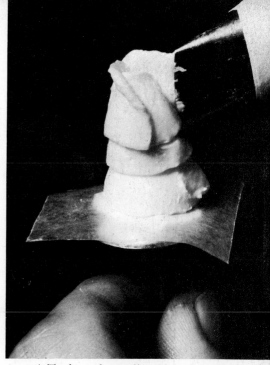

3 Rotating the nail slowly as you work, squeeze out a second icing cone about halfway up the sides of the first cone. Wipe the tip of the tube after each step.

4 To shape the small petals at the center, hold the end of the tube horizontal to the wax paper and squeeze three overlapping bands of icing around the second cone.

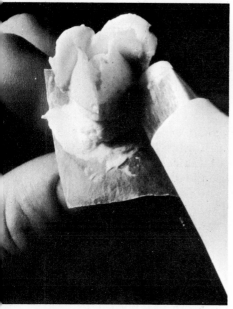

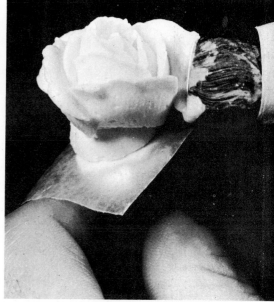

5 Squeeze out a second row of three petals just below the first row, turning the tube away from the cone as you work so that the petals stand out slightly.

6 Complete the rose with four large petals. Place the tube almost parallel to the paper; lift the tube up and out so that each petal curves away from the rose.

Sheath Cake

To make a 16-by-11-inch cake

CAKE

1 tablespoon butter, softened, plus
    ½ pound butter, cut into
    ¼-inch bits
2 tablespoons plus 2 cups unsifted
    flour
2 cups granulated sugar

¼ cup unsweetened cocoa
½ cup water
1 cup buttermilk
2 eggs, lightly beaten
1 teaspoon baking soda
1 teaspoon vanilla extract

Preheat the oven to 400°. With a pastry brush, spread the tablespoon of softened butter over the bottom and sides of a 16-by-11-inch jelly-roll pan. Add 2 tablespoons of the flour and tip the pan from side to side to distribute it evenly. Invert the pan and rap the bottom sharply to remove the excess flour. Set the pan aside.

Combine the remaining 2 cups of flour and the granulated sugar and sift them into a deep bowl. In a small heavy saucepan, combine the ¼ cup of cocoa with the water and stir with a wire whisk until the mixture is smooth. Add the ½ pound of butter bits, place the pan over moderate heat and whisk until the mixture comes to a boil and the butter is completely melted. Remove the pan from the heat and let the cocoa mixture cool for 2 or 3 minutes. Then, stirring constantly with the whisk, pour the cocoa mixture over the flour-and-sugar mixture in a slow, thin stream. When the batter is smooth, stir in the buttermilk, eggs, baking soda and 1 teaspoon of vanilla extract.

Pour the batter into the prepared pan and smooth the top with a spatula. Bake in the middle of the oven for about 20 minutes, or until a toothpick or cake tester inserted in the center comes out clean. Remove the cake from the oven and set it aside in the pan.

FROSTING

3½ cups confectioners' sugar
½ cup finely chopped pecans
¼ cup unsweetened cocoa
10 tablespoons light cream

8 tablespoons (1 quarter-pound
    stick) butter, cut into ¼-inch
    bits
1 teaspoon vanilla extract

To prepare the frosting, mix the confectioners' sugar and pecans together in a bowl. Combine ¼ cup of cocoa and the light cream in a small heavy saucepan and stir vigorously with a whisk until the mixture is smooth. Add the 8 tablespoons of butter bits, place the pan over moderate heat, and whisk until the mixture comes to a boil and the butter is completely melted.

Stirring constantly with the whisk, immediately pour the boiling cocoa mixture over the sugar-and-pecan mixture in a slow, thin stream. When the frosting is smooth, beat in 1 teaspoon of vanilla extract. Pour the frosting over the hot cake and spread it smooth with a rubber spatula.

Let the cake cool completely to room temperature before cutting it into squares or rectangles for serving.

Houston Gingerbread

To make a 13-by-9-inch cake

9 tablespoons butter, softened
2 tablespoons plus 2 cups unsifted flour
1 tablespoon unsweetened cocoa
2 teaspoons baking soda
2 teaspoons ground cinnamon
1½ teaspoons ground ginger
¼ teaspoon ground nutmeg
1 cup sugar
2 egg yolks
1 cup dark molasses
1 cup buttermilk
2 egg whites

Preheat the oven to 350°. With a pastry brush, spread 1 tablespoon of the softened butter over the bottom and sides of a 13-by-9-by-2-inch baking pan. Add 2 tablespoons of the flour and tip the pan from side to side to distribute it evenly. Invert the pan and rap the bottom sharply to remove the excess flour.

Combine the remaining 2 cups of flour, the cocoa, baking soda, cinnamon, ginger and nutmeg, and sift them into a bowl. Set aside.

In a deep bowl, cream the remaining 8 tablespoons of softened butter and the sugar together by beating and mashing them against the sides of the bowl with the back of a large spoon until the mixture is light and fluffy. Beat in the egg yolks, one at a time, and add the molasses. Add about ½ cup of the flour mixture and, when it is well incorporated, beat in about ¼ cup of the buttermilk. Repeat three times, alternating ½ cup of the flour mixture with ¼ cup of the buttermilk and beating the batter well after each addition.

With a wire whisk or a rotary or electric beater, beat the egg whites until they are stiff enough to stand in unwavering peaks on the beater when it is lifted from the bowl. With a rubber spatula, scoop the whites over the batter and fold them together gently but thoroughly.

Pour the batter into the prepared pan, spreading it evenly and smoothing the top with the spatula. Bake in the middle of the oven for about 25 minutes, or until a toothpick or cake tester inserted in the center comes out clean. Remove the gingerbread from the oven and let it cool completely to room temperature before cutting and serving it.

German's Chocolate Cake with Coconut Frosting

To make a 3-layer 9-inch cake

CAKE

3 tablespoons plus ½ pound
  butter, softened
6 tablespoons all-purpose flour
½ cup water
6 ounces (1½ bars) German's
  sweet chocolate, broken into
  ½-inch bits
2½ cups cake flour (not the self-

rising variety), sifted before
  measuring
1 teaspoon baking soda
½ teaspoon salt
1¾ cups sugar
4 egg yolks
1½ teaspoons vanilla extract
1 cup buttermilk
4 egg whites

German's chocolate is a blend of chocolate, cocoa butter and sugar, originally developed in 1852 in candy-bar form by Samuel German, an employee of Walter Baker & Company.

First prepare the cake in the following manner: Preheat the oven to 350°. With a pastry brush spread 3 tablespoons of the softened butter evenly over the bottom and sides of three 9-inch layer-cake pans. Add 2 tablespoons of the all-purpose flour to each pan and tip the pans from side to side to distribute the flour evenly. Invert the pans and rap the bottoms sharply to remove the excess flour. Set them aside.

Bring the water to a boil in a small saucepan and drop in the 6 ounces of chocolate bits. Stirring constantly, cook over low heat until the chocolate melts and the mixture is smooth. Remove the pan from the heat and let the chocolate mixture cool to room temperature.

Combine the cake flour, baking soda and salt, sift them into a bowl, and set the bowl aside.

In a deep bowl, cream the remaining ½ pound of softened butter and 1¾ cups of sugar together by beating and mashing them against the sides of the bowl with the back of a spoon until the mixture is light and fluffy. Beat in 4 egg yolks one at a time, and add 1½ teaspoons of vanilla.

Stirring the batter constantly, pour in the chocolate mixture in a slow, thin stream and continue to beat until the batter is smooth. Add about ½ cup of the cake-flour mixture and, when it is well incorporated, beat in ¼ cup of the buttermilk. Repeat three times, alternating about ½ cup of the flour mixture with ¼ cup of buttermilk and beating the batter well after each addition.

With a wire whisk or a rotary or electric beater, beat the egg whites until they are stiff enough to stand in unwavering peaks on the beater when it is lifted from the bowl. With a rubber spatula, scoop the egg whites over the batter and fold them together gently but thoroughly.

Pour the batter into the prepared pans, dividing it equally among them and smoothing the tops with the spatula. Bake in the middle of the oven for about 35 minutes, or until a toothpick or cake tester inserted in the centers comes out clean. Let the cakes cool in the pans for about 5 minutes, then turn them out on wire racks to cool completely to room temperature.

FROSTING
4 egg yolks
1 cup sugar
1 cup evaporated milk
12 tablespoons butter, cut into
    ½-inch bits and softened

2 ounces (½ bar) German's sweet
    chocolate, coarsely grated
1 teaspoon vanilla extract
A 4-ounce can sweetened shredded
    coconut (1⅓ cups)
1 cup coarsely chopped pecans

Meanwhile, prepare the frosting. With a wire whisk, beat 4 egg yolks and 1 cup of sugar together in a heavy 2- to 3-quart saucepan for 1 or 2 minutes. When the mixture is smooth and light, whisk in the evaporated milk. Add 12 tablespoons of softened butter bits and 2 ounces of grated chocolate, and set the pan over low heat. Stirring constantly with a large metal spoon, cook the mixture for 5 to 10 minutes, or until it is smooth and thick enough to cling lightly to the spoon. Do not let the mixture come anywhere near a boil or the egg yolks will curdle. Remove the pan from the heat and stir in 1 teaspoon of vanilla, the coconut and pecans.

Let the frosting cool to room temperature. Then refrigerate it for about 1 hour, stirring every 15 minutes, until the frosting holds its shape almost solidly in the spoon.

Place one layer of the cooled cake upside down on a serving plate and, with a metal spatula, spread the top with about one third of the frosting. Set the second layer in place, frost it, and add the third cake layer. Frost the top of the cake with all the remaining frosting (since the frosting is fragile, do not attempt to spread it on the sides of the cake).

Serve at once or refrigerate the cake until you are ready to serve it.

Buttermilk Poundcake

To make one 10-inch cake

1 tablespoon plus ½ pound butter,
  softened
2 tablespoons plus 2 cups unsifted
  flour
¼ teaspoon baking soda
½ teaspoon salt
2 cups sugar
4 egg yolks
⅔ cup buttermilk
1½ teaspoons lemon extract
4 egg whites
Confectioners' sugar (optional)

Preheat the oven to 350°. With a pastry brush, spread 1 tablespoon of the softened butter over the bottom and sides of a 10-inch tube cake pan. Add 2 tablespoons of the flour and tip the pan from side to side to distribute it evenly. Invert the pan and rap the bottom sharply to remove the excess flour. Combine the remaining 2 cups of flour, the baking soda and the salt, and sift them into a bowl. Set aside.

In a deep bowl, cream the remaining ½ pound of softened butter and the sugar together by beating and mashing them against the sides of the bowl with the back of a spoon until the mixture is light and fluffy. Beat in the egg yolks, one at a time. Add about ½ cup of the flour mixture and, when it is well incorporated, beat in about 3 tablespoons of the buttermilk. Repeat three times, alternating ½ cup of the flour mixture with 3 tablespoons of the buttermilk and beating well after each addition. Stir the lemon extract into the batter.

With a wire whisk or a rotary or electric beater, beat the egg whites until they are stiff enough to stand in unwavering peaks on the whisk or beater when it is lifted from the bowl. With a rubber spatula, scoop the egg whites over the batter and fold them together gently but thoroughly.

Pour the batter into the prepared pan and smooth the top with the spatula. Bake in the middle of the oven for 50 to 60 minutes, or until a toothpick or cake tester inserted in the center comes out clean. Let the cake cool in the pan for 5 minutes, then turn it out on a rack to cool completely.

Serve the buttermilk poundcake unfrosted. Or, if you prefer, sift a little confectioners' sugar over the top and sides of the cake before serving.

Postre Borracho
"DRUNKEN" CAKE

To make a 9-inch square cake

22 tablespoons (½ pound plus
   6 tablespoons) butter, softened
2 tablespoons plus 3⅓ cups sugar
2⅓ cups unsifted flour
1½ teaspoons double-acting
   baking powder
7 eggs, at room temperature
1 teaspoon vanilla extract
1 teaspoon almond extract
1 cup water
½ cup pure grain alcohol, or
   substitute ½ cup vodka

Preheat the oven to 350°. With a pastry brush, spread 1 tablespoon of the softened butter over the bottom and sides of a 9-inch square cake pan. Fit a square of wax paper into the bottom of the pan and brush the top with another tablespoon of softened butter. Sprinkle 2 tablespoons of the sugar over the buttered paper. Combine the flour and the baking powder and sift them into a bowl. Set aside.

In a deep bowl, cream the remaining 20 tablespoons of softened butter with 1⅓ cups of the sugar by beating and mashing them against the sides of the bowl with the back of a large spoon until the mixture is light and fluffy. Beat in the eggs, one at a time, and add the vanilla and almond extracts. Add the flour mixture to the batter ½ cup at a time, beating well after each addition.

Pour the batter into the prepared pan and smooth the top with a rubber spatula. Bake in the middle of the oven for about 50 minutes, or until a toothpick or cake tester inserted in the center comes out clean. Let the cake cool in the pan for about 5 minutes, then invert it onto a serving plate. Gently peel off the wax paper.

Meanwhile, combine the remaining 2 cups of sugar and the water in a small heavy saucepan. Stirring constantly, cook over low heat until the mixture comes to a boil and the sugar dissolves. Remove the pan from the heat and stir in the alcohol or vodka.

With a small skewer, pierce the cake all over, pressing the skewer completely through to the serving plate. Dribble the syrup over the cake and set aside at room temperature for about an hour before serving.

Pecan-stuffed Date Cookies

To make 45 cookies

COOKIES
6 tablespoons butter, softened
45 pitted dates (about 12 ounces)
45 shelled pecan halves (about
    4 ounces)
2 cups unsifted flour ·
½ teaspoon double-acting baking

powder
½ teaspoon baking soda
½ teaspoon salt
¾ cup light brown sugar
2 eggs
½ cup sour cream
1 teaspoon vanilla extract

Preheat the oven to 350°. With a pastry brush, spread 1 tablespoon of the softened butter evenly over each of two large baking sheets. Gently pry each date open along the slit in its side, insert a pecan half and press the edges of the date securely together. Set aside.

Combine the flour, baking powder, soda and salt, and sift them together into a bowl. In a deep mixing bowl, cream the remaining 4 tablespoons of softened butter with the brown sugar by beating and mashing them against the sides of the bowl with the back of a large spoon until the mixture is light and fluffy. Beat in the eggs, one at a time. Add 1 cup of the flour mixture and, when it is thoroughly incorporated, beat in ¼ cup of the sour cream. Repeat, alternating 1 cup of the flour with ¼ cup of sour cream and beating the batter well after each addition. Stir in 1 teaspoon of vanilla extract.

With kitchen tongs or your fingers, pick up one pecan-stuffed date at a time and swirl it in the batter to coat the entire surface evenly. As they are coated, arrange the dates about 1 inch apart on the buttered baking sheets. Bake in the middle of the oven for about 10 minutes, until the coating is delicately browned. Then transfer the cookies to wire racks to cool to room temperature.

ICING
8 tablespoons butter, cut into
    ½-inch bits

3 cups confectioners' sugar
1 tablespoon vanilla extract
3 to 4 tablespoons milk

When the cookies are cool, prepare the icing in the following fashion: Melt the 8 tablespoons of butter bits over low heat in a small heavy skillet, stirring so that the bits melt evenly without burning. Pour the melted butter into a mixing bowl and, when it has cooled, sift in the confectioners' sugar. Mix well, then stir in 1 tablespoon of vanilla extract and 3 tablespoons of milk. If the icing is too stiff to spread easily, add up to 1 tablespoon more milk by the teaspoonful.

With a small metal spatula, spread the icing evenly over the entire outside surface of each of the stuffed-date cookies and arrange them side by side on wax paper to dry. In a tightly covered jar or tin, the cookies may safely be kept for about 2 weeks.

Pecan Tassies

To make about 2 dozen miniature
   tarts

CRUST
1 cup unsifted flour
8 tablespoons butter, chilled and cut
   into ¼-inch bits

A 3-ounce package cream cheese,
   cut into ¼-inch bits and
   softened

Preheat the oven to 350°. Combine the flour and butter bits in a bowl and, with your fingertips, rub them together until the mixture resembles flakes of coarse meal. Add the cream cheese and continue to rub until the dough is smooth. Shape into a ball, wrap in wax paper and refrigerate the dough for at least 1 hour.

Pecan tassies are baked in a miniature muffin pan with 12 cups, each 1¾ inches across the top and ¾ inch deep. To make a pastry shell, cut off about 1 tablespoon of the dough and press it firmly into the bottom and against the sides of an ungreased muffin cup; repeat the process until you have filled two muffin pans. Smooth the inside surface of the pastry shells with a pestle or the bottom of a small glass.

FILLING
2 eggs
1 cup dark brown sugar
2 tablespoons butter, melted and
   cooled

1 teaspoon vanilla extract
⅛ teaspoon salt
½ cup finely chopped pecans
24 shelled pecan halves (about
   2 ounces)

To prepare the filling, beat the eggs lightly with a wire whisk or a rotary or electric beater. Beat in the brown sugar ½ cup at a time, then add the cooled melted butter and the vanilla extract and salt.

Place 1 teaspoon of chopped pecans in the bottom of a pastry shell, pour in about 1 tablespoon of filling, and set a pecan half on top. Bake the tarts in the middle of the oven for 15 to 20 minutes, or until the filling has puffed slightly and the top begins to crack. The filling will be somewhat firm to the touch.

Turn the pecan tassies out on wire racks to cool completely to room temperature before serving them.

Pecan Drops

To make about 2 dozen cookies

1 tablespoon butter, softened
1 egg white

1 cup light brown sugar, sifted
1½ cups pecan halves (about 6
ounces)

Preheat the oven to 250°. With a pastry brush, spread the softened butter evenly over two large baking sheets and set them aside.

With a wire whisk or a rotary or electric beater, beat the egg white until it is stiff enough to form soft peaks on the whisk or beater when it is lifted from the bowl. Beat in the brown sugar about ¼ cup at a time, and continue to beat until the meringue mixture is very stiff and no longer glossy. With a rubber spatula, gently fold in the pecan halves.

To form each pecan drop, scoop up 1 tablespoonful of the meringue mixture and, with the aid of another spoon, slide it in a small mound onto the buttered baking sheets. Arrange the pecan drops about 1 inch apart to allow them to spread slightly. Bake in the middle of the oven for about 30 minutes, or until the pecan drops have lost all their sheen and are a pale biscuit color. With a spatula, transfer them to a cake rack to cool before serving.

Fig Squares

To make about 4 dozen 1½-inch
squares

1 tablespoon butter, softened
2 tablespoons plus ¾ cup unsifted
flour
1 teaspoon double-acting baking
powder
¼ teaspoon ground cloves
¼ teaspoon ground cinnamon

¼ teaspoon salt
3 eggs
1 cup sugar
1 teaspoon vanilla extract
2 cups finely chopped dried figs
(about 16 ounces)
1 cup finely chopped walnuts
Confectioners' sugar

Preheat the oven to 325°. With a pastry brush, spread the softened butter over the bottom and sides of a 13-by-9-by-2-inch baking pan. Add 2 tablespoons of the flour and tip the pan from side to side to distribute it evenly. Then invert the pan and rap the bottom sharply to remove the excess flour. Combine the remaining ¾ cup of flour, the baking powder, cloves, cinnamon and salt, and sift them together into a bowl. Set aside.

In a deep bowl, beat the eggs with a wire whisk or a rotary or electric beater until they are smooth. Add the sugar and the flour mixture, about

½ cup at a time, beating well after each addition. Stir in the vanilla extract, figs and nuts.

Pour the batter into the prepared pan and smooth the top with a rubber spatula. Bake in the middle of the oven for about 25 minutes, or until the top is delicately browned and firm to the touch. Remove the pan from the oven and let the baked fig cake cool to room temperature. With a sharp knife, cut the cake into individual 1½-inch squares. Sift a little confectioners' sugar evenly over the squares.

Lollies

To make about 4 dozen 1½-inch
  square cookies

9 tablespoons butter, softened
1½ cups dark brown sugar
1 cup unsifted flour
2 eggs

½ teaspoon double-acting baking
  powder
½ teaspoon vanilla extract
1 cup finely chopped pecans
1 cup canned shredded coconut

First prepare the cookie base in the following manner: Preheat the oven to 375°. With a pastry brush, spread 1 tablespoon of the softened butter evenly over the bottom of a 13-by-9-by-2-inch cake pan and set it aside.

In a deep bowl, cream the remaining 8 tablespoons of butter and ½ cup of the dark brown sugar together by beating and mashing them against the sides of the bowl with the back of a large spoon until the mixture is light and fluffy. Beat in the flour ½ cup at a time. Place the mixture in the buttered pan and, with your fingers, pat it smooth. Bake in the middle of the oven for 15 minutes, or until the cookie base is delicately colored and firm to the touch.

Meanwhile, beat the eggs, baking powder and vanilla extract together lightly with a wire whisk or a fork. Add the remaining cup of brown sugar and mix well, then stir in the pecans and coconut.

When the cookie base has baked its allotted time, pour the egg batter over it and smooth the top with the back of a spoon. Continue baking for 15 minutes longer, or until the top is golden brown and firm. Remove the pan from the oven and let the cake cool completely to room temperature, then cut it into 1½-inch squares for serving.

Glass Cookies

To make 7 to 8 dozen 3-inch cookies

3½ cups unsifted flour
1 teaspoon ground nutmeg
½ teaspoon salt
2 cups sugar

12 tablespoons butter, softened
8 tablespoons vegetable shortening
2 eggs
1 teaspoon vanilla extract

Preheat the oven to 400°. Combine the flour, nutmeg and salt, and sift them together into a bowl. Place 1 cup of the sugar in another bowl and set it aside.

In a deep bowl, cream the butter, the shortening and the remaining cup of sugar together by beating and mashing them against the sides of the bowl with the back of a large spoon until the mixture is light and fluffy. Beat in the eggs, one at a time, and add the vanilla extract. Add the flour mixture by the cupful, beating well after each addition.

For each cookie, roll about 1 tablespoon of dough between your hands into a ball about 1 inch in diameter. Arrange the balls about 4 inches apart on ungreased cookie sheets. Dip the bottom of a glass 3 inches in diameter into the reserved bowl of sugar and press it down on a cookie ball. Repeat, dipping the bottom of the glass into sugar each time, until all the balls are flattened into 3-inch rounds and topped with sugar.

Bake the cookies in the middle of the oven for 7 to 8 minutes, or until the edges are delicately browned and crisp. Transfer the cookies to wire racks and let them cool to room temperature before serving. In a tightly covered jar or tin, the glass cookies can safely be kept for 2 or 3 weeks.

Almond-topped Cookies

To make about 3½ dozen 3-inch
   round cookies

2 cups unsifted flour
1¼ cups sugar
¼ teaspoon salt
½ pound butter, chilled and cut
   into ¼-inch bits, plus 2

teaspoons butter, softened
1 egg yolk
1 teaspoon vanilla extract
½ cup finely chopped almonds
1 egg white, lightly beaten

Combine the flour, 1 cup of the sugar and the salt in a deep bowl. Add the ½ pound of butter bits and, with your fingertips, rub the flour and fat together until the mixture resembles flakes of coarse meal. Add the egg yolk and vanilla extract, and stir with a large spoon until the dough is smooth and can be gathered into a compact ball. Pat and shape the dough into a cylinder 2½ to 3 inches in diameter, wrap in wax paper and refrigerate it for at least 1 hour.

Preheat the oven to 350°. With a pastry brush, spread the 2 teaspoons of softened butter evenly over two large baking sheets. Mix the remaining ¼ cup of sugar with the chopped almonds and set aside.

Using a large sharp knife, cut the dough into ¼-inch-thick rounds and arrange them about 1 inch apart on the buttered sheets. Brush the cookies lightly with the beaten egg white and sprinkle them evenly with the almond-sugar mixture.

Bake in the middle of the oven for about 10 minutes, or until the edges of the cookies are delicately browned. Transfer the cookies to wire racks and cool them to room temperature before serving.

Oatmeal Cookies

To make about 7 or 8 dozen 2-inch
   cookies

½ pound butter, softened	1½ cups unsifted flour
1 cup granulated sugar	1 teaspoon baking soda
1 cup dark brown sugar	1 teaspoon salt
2 eggs	3 cups quick-cooking oatmeal
1 teaspoon vanilla extract	½ cup finely chopped walnuts

In a deep bowl, cream the butter and the granulated and dark brown sugar together by beating and mashing them against the sides of the bowl with the back of a large spoon until the mixture is light and fluffy. Beat in the eggs, one at a time, and add the vanilla extract. Combine the flour, baking soda and salt in a sifter and sift them together directly into the bowl. Stir vigorously until the batter is smooth, then mix in the oatmeal by the cupful. Stir in the walnuts. Divide the dough in half and, on a lightly floured surface, roll each half into a cylinder about 2 inches in diameter and 14 to 15 inches long. Wrap the cylinders in wax paper and refrigerate for at least 12 hours or overnight.

Preheat the oven to 350°. With a sharp knife, cut the cylinders of dough crosswise into rounds about ⅓ inch thick. Arrange the rounds 1 inch apart on ungreased baking sheets and bake in the middle of the oven for 8 to 10 minutes, or until cookies are delicately browned and firm to the touch. Transfer them to wire racks and cool them to room temperature before serving. In tightly covered jars or tins, the oatmeal cookies can safely be kept for 2 or 3 weeks.

Bizcochuelos
LICORICE COOKIES

To make about 60 cookies

2½ cups unsifted flour	1 whole egg plus 1 egg yolk
½ teaspoon salt	1 tablespoon anise seed
1 cup lard	½ teaspoon anise extract
¾ cup sugar	4 tablespoons butter, softened

Combine the flour and salt, sift them into a bowl and set aside. In a deep bowl, cream the lard and the sugar together by beating and mashing them against the sides of the bowl with the back of a large spoon until the mixture is light and fluffy. Beat in the egg and egg yolk, then add the anise seed and anise extract. Beat in the flour mixture about ½ cup at a time. If the dough becomes too stiff to stir easily, incorporate the remaining flour mixture with your hands. Pat and shape the dough into two cylinders, each about 1½ inches in diameter. Wrap them in wax paper and refrigerate them for at least 1 hour.

Preheat the oven to 350°. With a pastry brush, spread 2 tablespoons of the softened butter evenly over two large baking sheets.

Slice one cylinder of dough crosswise into ¼-inch-thick rounds. For each cookie, roll a slice between your palms until it forms a rope about 4 inches long and ¼ inch in diameter. Drape the rope into a loop on a buttered baking sheet and cross the ends so that the loop looks like a hand-written letter "l." Arrange the cookies 1 inch apart to allow room for them to spread slightly. Bake in the middle of the oven for 10 to 12 minutes, or until the cookies are delicately browned. With a wide metal spatula, transfer them to wire racks.

Let the baking sheets cool completely and spread them with the remaining 2 tablespoons of softened butter. Then cut, shape and bake the remaining cookies in the same fashion. In a tightly covered jar or box, the *bizcochuelos* can safely be kept for 2 to 3 weeks.

C Lazy U Doughnuts

To make about 1½ dozen
   doughnuts and 4 to 5 dozen
   doughnut balls

3½ to 4½ cups unsifted flour
1 tablespoon double-acting baking
   powder
1 teaspoon ground cinnamon
½ teaspoon ground nutmeg
1 teaspoon salt

2 eggs
2 tablespoons butter, melted and
   cooled
1 cup sugar
1 cup milk
Vegetable oil for deep frying

Combine 3½ cups of flour with the baking powder, cinnamon, nutmeg and salt, and sift them into a bowl. Set aside.

In a deep bowl, beat the eggs lightly with a wire whisk. Whisking constantly, add the melted butter and the sugar. Add about 1 cup of the flour mixture and beat vigorously with a wooden spoon, then stir in ⅓ cup of the milk. Repeat two times, alternating about 1 cup of the flour mixture with ⅓ cup of milk and beating well after each addition. Cover the bowl with wax paper and refrigerate the dough for about 30 minutes.

Line one or two large baking sheets with wax paper. Cut off about half of the dough and place it on a lightly floured surface. Brush a rolling pin with flour and roll the dough out about ½ inch thick. If the dough sticks, dust a little flour over and under it. With a 2¾-inch doughnut cutter, cut out as many doughnuts as you can and, using a wide metal spatula, transfer them to the paper-lined pans.

Do not reroll the scraps, for the doughnuts made from them may be tough. Instead, use a 1-inch cutter to form balls out of the scraps and add these and the balls from the centers of the doughnuts to the lined pans. Refrigerate until ready to fry. Repeat the entire procedure with the remaining half of the dough, rolling it out as before and cutting as many doughnuts and balls as you can.

Pour oil into a deep fryer or a large heavy saucepan to a depth of about 3 inches and heat the oil to a temperature of 375° on a deep-frying thermometer. Deep-fry the doughnuts three or four at a time and the balls seven or eight at a time. Turn them with a slotted spoon for about 3 minutes, or until they are puffed and brown. As they brown, transfer the doughnuts and balls to paper towels to drain.

Serve the C Lazy U doughnuts warm or at room temperature.

Lemon Bars

To make about 32 two-by-one-inch
 bars

9 tablespoons butter, softened
1¼ cups confectioners' sugar
1 cup plus 2 tablespoons unsifted
 flour
1 cup granulated sugar
½ teaspoon double-acting baking
 powder
2 eggs
4 to 5 tablespoons strained fresh
 lemon juice
2 teaspoons finely grated fresh
 lemon peel

First prepare the base in the following manner: Preheat the oven to 350°. With a pastry brush, spread 1 tablespoon of the softened butter evenly over the bottom of an 8-inch square cake pan. Set it aside.

In a deep bowl, cream the remaining 8 tablespoons of butter and ¼ cup of the confectioners' sugar together by beating and mashing them against the sides of the bowl with the back of a large spoon until the mixture is light and fluffy. Beat in 1 cup of the flour ½ cup at a time. Place the mixture in the buttered pan and, with your fingers, pat it smooth. Bake in the middle of the oven for 15 minutes, or until the cookie base is delicately colored and firm to the touch.

Meanwhile, combine the granulated sugar, the remaining 2 tablespoons of flour and the baking powder, and sift them into a bowl. Add the eggs and beat vigorously with a spoon until the mixture is smooth. Stir in 2 tablespoons of the lemon juice and the 2 teaspoons of lemon peel.

When the cookie base has baked its allotted time, pour the egg batter over it and smooth the top with the back of the spoon. Continue baking for about 25 minutes longer, or until the top is golden brown and firm. Remove the pan from the oven and let cool to room temperature.

To prepare the icing: Combine the remaining cup of confectioners' sugar and 2 tablespoons of lemon juice in a bowl and mix well. If the icing is stiff, stir in up to 1 tablespoon more lemon juice by the teaspoonful until the icing becomes creamy enough to spread. With a rubber spatula, scoop the icing onto the cooled lemon-bar cake and spread it evenly over the top.

Set the lemon-bar cake aside for about 15 minutes, until the icing hardens, then cut the cake into 2-by-1-inch bars. Drape foil or wax paper over the pan and let the lemon bars rest at room temperature for about a day before serving them. The three layers—cookie base, lemon topping and icing—will blend with one another and give the lemon bars the chewy, somewhat sticky consistency of gumdrops.

MEXICAN-AMERICAN DISHES

Recipes with Spanish titles that appear in other sections of the Recipe Booklet did not evolve through Mexican or Border cooking, but were influenced directly by cooks from Old Spain.

All-Day Beans

To serve 4 to 6

2 cups (1 pound) dried pinto beans
6 cups water
A 2-ounce piece of lean salt pork, with the rind removed
4 dried hot red chilies, each about 1 inch long, stemmed, seeded if desired, and pulverized in a blender or with a mortar and pestle *(caution: see note, page 3)*
1 medium-sized onion, peeled and thinly sliced
1 teaspoon salt
1 recipe *salsa cruda (page 133)*

Wash the beans in a colander set under cold running water and discard any blemished beans. In a heavy 3- to 4-quart saucepan, bring the water to a boil over high heat. Drop in the beans and cook briskly, uncovered, for 2 minutes. Then turn off the heat and let the beans soak for 1 hour.

Add the salt pork, chilies and onion slices, and bring the mixture to a boil over high heat. Reduce the heat to its lowest setting and simmer tightly covered for 5½ hours. Stir in the salt and simmer for 30 minutes longer, or until a bean can be easily mashed against the side of the pan with the back of a spoon. (Stir the beans from time to time. If the water seems to be cooking away, add more boiling water by the ¼ cup. When fully cooked, however, the beans should have absorbed most of the liquid.)

Ladle the all-day beans into individual heated bowls and mound a teaspoon of *salsa cruda* on top of each portion. Spoon the remaining *salsa cruda* into a separate bowl and serve it at once with the beans.

Refried Beans

To serve 4 to 6

2 cups (1 pound) dried pinto or kidney beans
6 cups water
1 cup coarsely chopped onions
2 medium-sized firm ripe tomatoes, peeled, seeded and coarsely chopped (*see chile con queso,* *page 8*) or ⅔ cup chopped, drained canned tomatoes
1½ teaspoons finely chopped garlic
8 tablespoons lard
1 teaspoon salt
Sour cream (optional)

Under cold running water, wash the beans in a sieve or colander until the draining water runs clear. Pick out and discard any black or shriveled beans. Combine the beans, the 6 cups of water, ½ cup of the onions, ¼ cup of the tomatoes, the garlic and 1 tablespoon of lard in a heavy 3- to 4-quart saucepan. Bring to a boil over high heat, reduce the heat to low, cover the pan partially, and simmer for 1½ hours. Stir in the salt and continue to simmer partially covered for 30 to 40 minutes, or until a bean can be easily mashed against the side of the pan with the back of a spoon. (Check the pot from time to time and stir the beans gently. If the water seems to be boiling away, add more boiling water by the ¼ cup. When fully cooked, however, the beans should have absorbed most of the liquid.) Drain the beans in a sieve or colander set over a bowl and reserve the cooking liquid.

In a heavy 12-inch skillet, melt 2 tablespoons of the lard over moderate heat until a light haze forms above it. Add the remaining ½ cup of onions and, stirring frequently, cook for about 5 minutes, until they are soft and translucent but not brown. Add the remaining chopped tomatoes and stir for 2 to 3 minutes. Reduce the heat to low.

Fry the beans in the following manner: Add about ½ cup of the beans to the skillet, mash them flat with a table fork and stir in 1 tablespoon of the remaining lard. Repeat, alternating about 1 cup of the beans with 1 tablespoon of the lard until all the beans and lard have been mashed together. The bean mixture should be moist and creamy. If it appears dry, beat in the reserved cooking liquid by the tablespoonful, adding only enough to achieve the texture you desire.

Mound the refried beans in a heated serving bowl or individual dishes and serve at once, accompanied if you like by a separate bowl of sour cream. Refried beans are also used as filling for enchiladas or tacos.

Bocoles
CORN-FLOUR-AND-BEAN CAKES

To serve 4 to 8

2 cups instant *masa harina* (corn flour)
½ teaspoon salt
1 cup water
½ cup mashed drained freshly cooked or canned pinto beans
2 tablespoons vegetable oil
8 freshly fried eggs

1 pound freshly fried crumbled homemade *chorizo* sausage meat *(page 122)*, or substitute 1 pound commercial *chorizo* sausages, skinned, crumbled and fried
Salsa cruda (page 133), fresh red chili sauce *(page 73)* or green-chili sauce *(page 126)*

Bocoles, a Texas-coined word that may be translated as "mouth-watering," is used to describe corn-flour-and-bean cakes that are traditionally topped with fried eggs, sausage meat and hot sauce to make a popular breakfast or lunch dish.

Combine the *masa harina* and salt in a deep bowl and, stirring constantly with a large spoon, pour in the water in a slow, thin stream. Add the mashed beans and beat vigorously with the spoon, or knead with your hands, until the dough is no longer sticky but is firm.

Divide the dough into eight equal parts and shape each part into a flat round cake about 2½ inches in diameter and ½ inch thick. In a heavy 12-inch skillet, heat the oil over moderate heat until a light haze forms above it. Fry the cakes for about 4 minutes on each side, turning them with a spatula when the bottoms are crisp and flecked with brown.

To serve, place the *bocoles* on heated individual plates and cover each cake with a fried egg. Spoon the crumbled sausage meat over and around the eggs and top each serving with a little *salsa cruda* or chili sauce. Ladle the rest of the sauce into a sauceboat or small bowl and serve it separately with the *bocoles*.

Green Corn Tamales

To make 30 tamales

6 large ears of corn
1½ cups freshly grated Monterey Jack, longhorn or Cheddar cheese
A 4-ounce can green chilies (not the *jalapeño* variety), drained, halved, seeded and finely chopped
2 teaspoons salt
⅛ teaspoon ground white pepper
12 tablespoons (¾ cup) lard
3½ cups instant *masa harina* (corn flour)
2 cups warm water

Shuck the corn carefully so that the husks do not tear, dropping the husks into a large pot of cold water as you proceed. Spread the husks on paper towels to drain, pat them completely dry with fresh towels, and set aside. Pull off and discard the cornsilk, then cut the kernels from the cobs with a sharp knife and discard the cobs.

Place about one third of the corn kernels in the jar of an electric blender and blend at low speed for 30 seconds. Turn off the machine, scrape down the sides of the jar with a rubber spatula, and blend again until the corn is a rough purée. Scrape the purée into a deep bowl, and blend the remaining corn in two batches, following the same procedure.

Add the cheese, chilies, 1 teaspoon of the salt and the white pepper to the corn purée, mix well, and set aside.

In a deep bowl, cream the lard by beating and mashing it against the sides of the bowl with the back of a large spoon until the lard is light and fluffy. Add the remaining teaspoon of salt, then beat in the *masa harina* by the cupful. Stirring the mixture constantly with a spoon, pour in the 2 cups of warm water in a slow, thin stream; continue to beat for 4 or 5 minutes, until a soft, moist dough is formed.

To assemble each green corn tamale, spread out one of the cornhusks on a flat surface. The husk should be at least 4 inches wide; if necessary, place two cornhusks side by side, overlapping them to achieve the proper width. Place 2 tablespoons of the *masa harina* dough on the husk close to one long edge and 2 or 3 inches from the wide bottom end. With a spatula or the back of a fork, flatten the dough into a rectangle about 2 inches wide and 3 inches long and mound 2 tablespoons of the corn-chili mixture on top of it. Following the drawings opposite, fold the long sides of the husk over the filling, then turn up and overlap the ends. (At this stage the tamales may be wrapped in foil and kept in the freezer for up to 2 or 3 months. Defrost the tamales before cooking them.)

To cook the tamales, stack them in layers, seam side down, in a large colander. Set the colander inside a deep pot and pour enough water into the pot to come to within an inch of the bottom of the colander. Bring to a boil over high heat, cover the pot tightly and reduce the heat to low. Steam the tamales for 1 hour, keeping the water at a slow boil and replenishing it with boiling water as it evaporates.

Lift the tamales from the colander with tongs, arrange them attractively on a heated platter and serve at once.

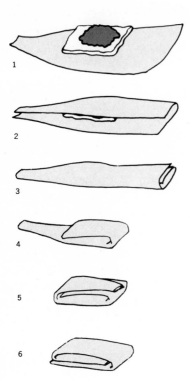

HOW TO FILL AND SHAPE
A GREEN CORN TAMALE

Flatten out a large cornhusk or overlap two smaller husks to make a wrapper 4 to 5 inches wide and at least 8 inches long. (1) Place 2 tablespoons of the *masa* dough along one edge of the husk in a rectangle about 2 inches wide and 3 inches long and spread the dough to that edge of the husk. Mound 2 tablespoons of the filling in the middle of the *masa*. (2) Fold over the *masa*-covered edge of the rectangle by about 1 inch and press it down to enclose the filling snugly. (3) Fold the other edge of the husk over the filled portion. (4) Fold the bottom of the husk over the filled portion. (5) Fold the top of the husk to form a neat rectangular package. (6) Turn the tamale seam side down to keep it in shape.

Corn Tortillas

To make 1 dozen 5-inch tortillas

2⅓ cups instant *masa harina* (corn flour)

1 teaspoon salt
1 to 1½ cups cold water

Combine the *masa harina* and salt in a deep bowl and, stirring the mixture constantly, pour in 1 cup of the water in a slow, thin stream. Then knead the mixture vigorously with your hands, adding up to ½ cup more water by the tablespoonful if necessary, until the dough becomes firm and no longer sticks to the fingers.

To shape the tortillas, divide the dough into 12 equal portions and roll each one between your palms into a ball the size of a walnut. Place one ball at a time between two 8-inch squares of wax paper, then flatten it into a 5- to 6-inch round in a tortilla press. Stack the tortillas on top of one another without removing the papers.

Preheat the oven to its lowest setting. Then heat an ungreased cast-iron griddle or a 7- to 8-inch cast-iron skillet over moderate heat until a drop of water flicked onto it splutters and evaporates instantly. Unwrap and fry one tortilla at a time for about 2 minutes on each side, turning it once with a spatula when the bottom becomes a delicate brown. Watch carefully and regulate the heat if the tortilla colors too quickly. As they brown, transfer the tortillas to a large platter. Wrap the tortillas in foil, four or five at a time, as you proceed, and keep them warm in the oven.

If you prefer, you may stack and wrap all of the tortillas together in paper towels, cover them with a damp cloth and finally with foil, then place them in the oven to keep warm for 2 to 3 hours.

To prepare tortillas days or weeks in advance, cook and cool them to room temperature. Stack them between pieces of wax paper and wrap the stack with foil. Tightly wrapped, the tortillas can safely be kept in the refrigerator for 2 or 3 days, or in the freezer for months. To rewarm the refrigerated tortillas, unwrap one at a time and heat it in an ungreased skillet for about 30 seconds, turning the tortilla frequently with tongs until it softens and is heated through. Frozen tortillas should be thoroughly defrosted before they are reheated.

Chicken Tostadas
FRIED TORTILLAS TOPPED WITH CHICKEN AND LETTUCE

To serve 6

	8 whole black peppercorns
3 one-pound chicken breasts	2 teaspoons salt
1 medium-sized onion, peeled and	1 firm medium-sized head of iceberg
coarsely chopped	lettuce
¼ cup coarsely chopped celery,	6 to 8 tablespoons lard
including the leaves	12 corn tortillas *(opposite)*,
1 medium-sized bay leaf, crumbled	thoroughly defrosted if frozen
6 fresh parsley sprigs	Poor man's butter *(page 135)*

Place the chicken breasts in a heavy 4- to 5-quart saucepan and pour in enough water to cover them by at least 1 inch. Bring to a boil over high heat, meanwhile skimming off the foam and scum as they rise to the surface. Add the onion, celery, bay leaf, parsley, peppercorns and salt, then reduce the heat to low. Simmer the chicken partially covered for 20 to 30 minutes, or until the breasts have turned opaque and feel firm when prodded with a finger.

With a slotted spoon, transfer the chicken breasts to a plate, and discard the cooking liquid and seasonings. Remove the skin from the breasts with a small knife or your fingers. Cut or pull the meat away from the bones. Discard the skin and bones and cut the meat into strips about ⅛ inch wide and 1½ to 2 inches long.

Wash the head of lettuce under cold running water and remove the tough outer leaves. With a small sharp knife, cut out the core from the base of the head. To shred the lettuce, cut the head into quarters and slice the quarters crosswise into ⅛-inch-wide strips.

In a heavy 8- to 10-inch skillet, heat 2 tablespoons of the lard over moderate heat until it is very hot but not smoking. Add one tortilla and fry it for about 1 minute on each side, or until it is crisp and lightly browned. With tongs, transfer the fried tortilla (now a *tostada*) to paper towels to drain while you fry the remaining tortillas. Replenish the lard in the skillet as you proceed, adding it by the tablespoonful when necessary.

To assemble the *tostadas,* place two of them side by side on each of six heated serving plates. Scatter the chicken strips and shredded lettuce over the *tostadas,* dividing the chicken and lettuce equally among them. Mound a tablespoonful of the poor man's butter on top of each *tostada* and serve the rest in a bowl. Serve the chicken *tostadas* at once, accompanied if you like by red tomato taco sauce or *jalapeño* sauce *(page 134).*

Beef Tacos
DEEP-FRIED FOLDED TORTILLAS WITH BEEF FILLING

To make 8 tacos

Vegetable oil for deep frying
8 corn tortillas *(page 118)*, each
    5 to 6 inches across, thoroughly
    defrosted if frozen
3 tablespoons lard
1 pound lean ground beef

1 cup finely chopped onions
1 teaspoon salt
1 cup *ancho* sauce *(page 135)*
1 cup finely shredded iceberg lettuce
1 cup (about 4 ounces) coarsely
    shredded Cheddar or longhorn
    cheese

Pour vegetable oil into a deep fryer or large heavy saucepan to a depth of about 4 inches and heat the oil until it reaches a temperature of 350° on a deep-frying thermometer. At the same time, preheat the oven to its lowest setting. Line a jelly-roll pan with a double thickness of paper towels and place it in the middle of the oven.

Meanwhile, soften and warm the tortillas one at a time in an ungreased 10-inch skillet set over moderate heat. Turn the tortillas over and back with kitchen tongs for about 30 seconds, until they are soft but not browned. Stack them on a plate as you proceed.

To shape and fry the tortillas to make taco shells, fold two tortillas around the outside of the holders of a taco fryer and set the holders into place in the fryer *(photographs, opposite)*. Lower the holders into the hot oil by a wire and deep-fry the tortillas for 2 minutes, or until they are brown and crisp. As they are fried, transfer the completed taco shells to the lined pan and keep them warm in the oven.

In a heavy 10- to 12-inch skillet, melt the lard over moderate heat. Add the beef and fry it for 8 to 10 minutes, stirring frequently and mashing the meat with the back of a spoon to prevent lumps from forming. When no trace of pink remains, stir in ½ cup of the onions and the salt. Remove the pan from the heat, add ½ cup of the *ancho* sauce, and taste the beef mixture for seasoning.

Spoon the beef filling into the taco shells, dividing it evenly among them. Then arrange the tacos attractively on a heated platter and serve at once, accompanied by the shredded lettuce and cheese and the remaining chopped onions and *ancho* sauce in four separate bowls. For spicier tacos, you may also serve red tomato taco sauce *(page 134)*.

NOTE: Lacking a taco fryer, pour vegetable oil into a heavy 10- to 12-inch skillet to a depth of about 1 inch and heat the oil until it is very hot but not smoking. To shape each taco shell, fold a tortilla in half and carefully place it in the hot oil. As it fries, hold the tortilla slightly open with kitchen tongs or two forks so that there is about ½ inch of space between the halves. Fry the taco shell for 2 to 3 minutes, turning it over so that it is crisp and brown on both sides. As they brown, transfer the taco shells to the paper-lined pan and keep them warm in the oven while you fold and fry the rest.

HOW TO USE A TACO MAKER
A Molina taco maker *(see Shopping Guide, page 150)* has a metal frame shaped, in profile, somewhat like a W; each of the two V-shaped slots contains a removable metal tortilla holder. To make folded shells for beef tacos *(recipe, opposite)*, wrap a tortilla around the outside of each holder *(left)* and place it in a slot *(center)*. Holding the taco maker by its wire handle, carefully lower it into the hot oil *(right)*. Deep-fry the tortillas for about 2 minutes, then lift out the taco maker. Slide the holders out of the frame and gently slip off the fried tacos. Wrap two more tortillas around the holders and repeat the entire procedure until all the tacos have been folded and fried.

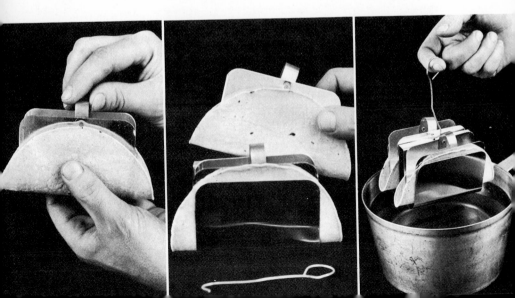

Tostaditas
DEEP-FRIED CORN CHIPS

Vegetable oil for deep frying   thoroughly defrosted if frozen
Corn tortillas *(page 118)*,   Salt

Pour vegetable oil into a deep fryer or large heavy saucepan to a depth of about 3 inches and heat the oil until it reaches a temperature of 375° on a deep-frying thermometer.

Cut the tortillas into 1- or 2-inch pieces with a sharp knife, or tear them apart with your fingers.

Deep-fry the tortilla pieces, 5 or 10 at a time depending on their size, turning them about with a slotted spoon for about a minute, or until they are crisp and brown on all sides. As they are fried, transfer the *tostaditas* to paper towels to drain.

When all the *tostaditas* are deep-fried and drained, sprinkle them lightly with salt. Serve the *tostaditas* as a snack or as an accompaniment to *chile con queso* or *guacamole (Recipe Index)*. Tightly covered, the *tostaditas* can safely be kept for 2 or 3 weeks.

Chorizo Flautas
ROLLED TORTILLAS WITH HOMEMADE SAUSAGE FILLING

To serve 6 to 8

HOMEMADE SAUSAGE
2 pounds lean pork, trimmed of
  excess fat, cut into ¼-inch-thick
  slices and coarsely chopped
3 tablespoons chili powder
2 tablespoons red wine vinegar
1 tablespoon finely chopped garlic
1 tablespoon crumbled dried

oregano
1½ teaspoons salt
2 tablespoons lard

Vegetable oil
32 corn tortillas *(page 118)*, each 5
  to 6 inches across, thoroughly
  defrosted if frozen
Fresh red chili sauce *(page 73)*

Combine the pork, chili powder, vinegar, garlic, oregano and salt in a bowl and knead vigorously with both hands, then beat with a large spoon until the sausage mixture is smooth.

In a heavy 10- to 12-inch skillet, melt the lard over moderate heat until a drop of water flicked into it splutters and evaporates instantly. Add the sausage mixture and fry for 8 to 10 minutes, stirring frequently and mashing the meat with the back of a spoon to prevent any lumps from forming. Do not let the sausage brown. When no trace of pink remains, taste the sausage for seasoning and remove the pan from the heat.

Pour vegetable oil into a 12-inch skillet to a depth of about 1 inch and heat the oil until it is very hot but not smoking. Meanwhile, warm the tortillas one at a time in an ungreased 10-inch skillet set over moderate heat. Turn the tortillas over and back with tongs for about 30 seconds, until they are soft but not browned. Stack them on a plate as you proceed.

To assemble each *flauta,* place two tortillas side by side on a flat surface, overlapping them by about 2 inches *(illustrations, below)*. Spoon ¼ cup of the warm sausage mixture onto the tortillas as shown. Fold the tortillas over the meat and roll them into a cylinder. Hold the *flauta* in shape with two or three wooden toothpicks.

Fry two or three *flautas* at a time in the hot oil, turning them over with a slotted spatula or tongs for about 2 minutes, or until they are crisp and golden. As they are done, transfer the *flautas* to paper towels to drain.

Arrange the *flautas* attractively on a heated platter and serve them while they are hot, accompanied by the red chili sauce in a separate bowl.

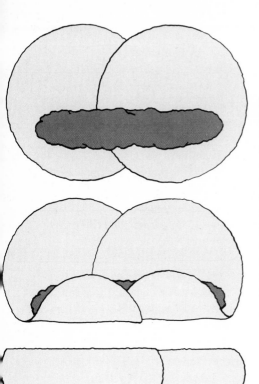

HOW TO FILL AND SHAPE A FLAUTA
Spread out two tortillas, overlapping them by about 2 inches, eclipse fashion. *Top:* Spoon ¼ cup of the filling across the lower half of the overlapping tortillas, forming a band about 1 inch wide and 8 inches long. *Center:* Fold the bottom edges of both tortillas up over the filling. *Bottom:* Starting at the filled edge, roll up the tortillas into a tight cylinder to enclose the filling. As the name suggests, a rolled *flauta* looks somewhat like a flute.

Enchiladas de Jocoque
TORTILLAS FILLED WITH CHICKEN AND SOUR CREAM

To serve 4

2 one-pound chicken breasts
2 cups water
1 medium-sized onion, peeled and
  coarsely chopped
¼ cup coarsely chopped celery
  leaves
1 small bay leaf, crumbled
4 fresh parsley sprigs
4 whole black peppercorns
1 teaspoon salt
3 cups sour cream
1 tablespoon butter, softened, plus
  2 tablespoons butter, cut into

small bits
¼ cup finely chopped onions
A 4-ounce can green chilies (not
  the *jalapeño* variety), drained
  and finely chopped
8 corn tortillas *(page 118)*,
  thoroughly defrosted if frozen
Eight 4-by-2-by-⅛-inch slices
  Monterey Jack or Münster cheese
8 pitted black olives, cut lengthwise
  into halves
Eight 2-by-¼-inch strips canned
  pimiento

Combine the chicken breasts and water in a heavy 3- to 4-quart saucepan and bring to a boil over high heat, skimming off the foam and scum as they rise to the surface. Add the coarsely chopped onion and the celery, bay leaf, parsley, peppercorns and salt, then reduce the heat to low. Simmer partially covered for 20 to 30 minutes, or until the breasts have turned opaque and feel firm when prodded with a finger.

With a slotted spoon, transfer the chicken breasts to a plate. Strain the cooking liquid through a fine sieve, pressing down hard on the seasonings with the back of a spoon to extract all their juices before discarding the pulp. Return the strained liquid to the pan and boil briskly, uncovered, until the stock is reduced to 1 cup. Taste for seasoning, pour the stock into a bowl, then mix in the sour cream and set aside.

When the chicken is cool enough to handle, remove the skin with a small knife or your fingers. Cut or pull the meat away from the bones. Discard the skin and bones and cut the meat into ½-inch cubes.

Preheat the oven to 375°. With a pastry brush, spread the tablespoon of softened butter evenly over the bottom and sides of a 13-by-9-by-2-inch baking dish and set the dish aside.

In a heavy 6- to 8-inch skillet, melt the 2 tablespoons of butter bits over moderate heat. When the foam begins to subside, add the finely chopped onions and, stirring frequently, cook for about 5 minutes, or until they are soft and translucent but not brown. Stir in the green chilies and, with a rubber spatula, transfer the entire contents of the skillet to a bowl. Add the cubed chicken and 1 cup of the reserved sour-cream-and-stock mixture and toss the ingredients together gently but thoroughly. Set the filling aside.

Soften the tortillas one at a time in an ungreased 10-inch skillet set over moderate heat. Turn each tortilla over and back with tongs for about 30 seconds, until it is soft but not browned.

To assemble each enchilada, lay a softened tortilla flat and spread about ⅓ cup of the chicken-and-sour-cream filling in a band on the lower third of the tortilla as shown below. Following the diagrams, fold up the bottom edge and roll the enchilada into a tight cylinder. Place the enchiladas side by side in two rows in the buttered dish and ladle the remaining sour-cream-and-stock mixture over them. Set a slice of cheese on each enchilada and arrange the black olive halves and pimiento strips decoratively over the top.

Bake in the middle of the oven for about 20 minutes, or until the cheese is melted and the sauce bubbly. Serve the *enchiladas de Jocoque* at once, directly from the baking dish.

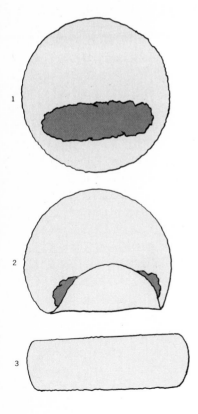

HOW TO FILL AND ROLL AN ENCHILADA DE JOCOQUE
For each *enchilada de Jocoque,* lay a softened tortilla flat and (1) spread ⅓ cup of filling over the lower third of the tortilla in a band about 3 inches long and 1 inch wide. (2) Fold the bottom edge of the tortilla up and over the filling to cover it almost completely. (3) Then, starting at the filled edge, roll the tortilla into a tight cylinder. It is neither traditional nor necessary to tuck in the ends of the enchilada.

Stacked Cheese Enchiladas, New Mexico Style

To serve 4

GREEN-CHILI SAUCE
2 tablespoons lard
½ cup finely chopped onions
An 8½-ounce can *tomatitos*
 (Mexican green tomatoes),
 drained and coarsely chopped

2 four-ounce cans green chilies
 (not the *jalapeño* variety),
 drained and finely chopped
 (about 1 cup)
½ cup light cream
1 teaspoon salt

First prepare the green-chili sauce in the following manner: In a heavy 8- to 10-inch skillet, melt the lard over moderate heat. Add the onions and stir frequently for about 5 minutes, or until they are soft and translucent but not brown. Add the *tomatitos* and mash them with the back of the spoon. Stir in the chilies, then add the cream. Stirring constantly, cook briskly until the sauce is thick enough to hold its shape almost solidly in the spoon. Add the salt and taste for seasoning. Remove the skillet from the heat. (There will be about 2 cups of sauce.)

ENCHILADAS
Vegetable oil
Twelve 5- to 6-inch corn tortillas
 (page 118), thoroughly
 defrosted if frozen
4 cups (1 pound) freshly grated
 Monterey Jack or Cheddar cheese

Preheat the broiler to its highest setting. Pour vegetable oil into a heavy 10-inch skillet to a depth of about 1 inch and heat the oil until it is very hot but not smoking. Pick up one tortilla at a time with kitchen tongs, immerse it in the oil for a few seconds to heat and soften it, and immediately transfer it to paper towels to drain.

To assemble each enchilada, place a hot tortilla on an ovenproof serving plate and spread 2 tablespoons of the chili sauce over it. Scatter about ¼ cup of cheese on top, add a second tortilla and cover it with chili sauce and cheese in the same fashion. Set a third tortilla on top, spread it with ¼ cup of chili sauce and scatter about ½ cup of cheese over it.

When all the enchiladas are assembled, slide them under the broiler for 30 seconds or so, to melt the cheese topping. Serve at once.

Wheat Tortillas

To make six 7-inch or two 15-inch
  tortillas

2 cups unsifted flour
½ teaspoon salt

4 tablespoons lard, cut into ½-inch
  bits
½ cup lukewarm water (110° to 115°)

Combine the flour and salt in a deep bowl. Add the lard and, with your fingertips, rub the flour and fat together until the mixture resembles flakes of coarse meal. Pour in the water and mix with your fingers or a spoon until the dough can be gathered into a ball. Set the dough aside at room temperature to rest for about 15 minutes.

To make small tortillas, divide the dough into six equal portions and, on a lightly floured surface, roll each of them out into a round about 7 inches in diameter and ⅛ inch thick. If you like, you can trim off the rough edges of the tortillas with a pastry wheel or sharp knife, using a 7-inch plate or pot lid as a guide.

Preheat the oven to its lowest setting. Then heat an ungreased 8- to 10-inch cast-iron skillet over moderate heat until a drop of water flicked onto it splutters and evaporates instantly. Fry one tortilla at a time for about a minute on each side, turning it with a spatula when the bottom is flecked with brown. Watch carefully and regulate the heat if the tortilla colors too quickly. As the tortillas brown, transfer them to a platter.

Wrap the tortillas in foil two or three at a time as you proceed, and keep them warm in the oven until the entire batch is cooked. If you prefer, you may wrap all the tortillas in paper towels, cover them with a damp cloth and foil, then keep them warm in the oven for 2 to 3 hours.

To make large tortillas, divide the dough in half and, on a lightly floured surface, roll each half into a 15- to 16-inch round about ⅛ inch thick. If you like, you can trim off the rough edges of the tortillas with a pastry wheel or sharp knife, using a 15-inch pizza pan as a pattern.

Preheat the oven to its lowest setting. At the same time, place an ungreased 15-inch pizza pan over moderate heat. Grasping pot holders in both hands, slide the pan back and forth until the entire surface is hot and a drop of water flicked onto it splutters and evaporates instantly. Fry one tortilla at a time for 2 to 3 minutes on each side, sliding the pan back and forth constantly and turning the tortilla once with a spatula when the bottom becomes flecked with brown. Watch carefully and regulate the heat if the tortilla colors too quickly. As the tortillas are cooked, transfer them to large platters.

Use the large tortillas at once or stack and wrap them together in paper towels, cover them with a damp cloth and finally with foil, and keep them warm in a low oven for 2 to 3 hours.

Small wheat tortillas are used as wrappers for *chimichangos* or *burritos (Recipe Index);* the large tortillas serve as the bases for Southwestern pizza *(page 133).*

Chimichangos Dulces
DEEP-FRIED WHEAT TORTILLAS WITH FRUIT FILLING

To make 12 *chimichangos*

TORTILLAS
4 cups unsifted flour
½ teaspoon ground cinnamon
1 teaspoon salt

8 tablespoons lard, cut into ½-inch
  bits
1 cup lukewarm water (110° to
  115°)

To make the wheat tortillas, combine the flour, cinnamon and salt in a deep bowl and, following the directions for wheat tortillas on page 127, mix in the lard and lukewarm water. Let the dough rest for about 15 minutes, then divide it into 12 equal portions and roll each one into a round about 7 inches in diameter and ⅛ inch thick. Fry the tortillas in an ungreased skillet and set them aside on a platter to cool.

FILLING
1 cup coarsely chopped dried apples
1 cup coarsely chopped dried
  apricots
1½ to 2 cups water
½ cup granulated sugar

½ teaspoon finely grated fresh
  lemon peel

4 tablespoons butter, softened
Vegetable oil for deep frying
Confectioners' sugar

Meanwhile, prepare the filling in the following fashion: Combine the apples, apricots and 1½ cups of water in a heavy 1- to 1½-quart saucepan and bring to a boil over high heat. Reduce the heat to low and simmer partially covered for about 20 minutes, or until the fruit is soft and the mixture is thick enough to hold its shape almost solidly in a spoon. (Check the pan from time to time and add up to ½ cup more water by the tablespoonful if necessary. When the fruit is fully cooked, however, it will have absorbed most of the liquid in the pan.) Transfer the fruit mixture to a bowl and stir in the granulated sugar and the lemon peel. Set the filling aside to cool to room temperature.

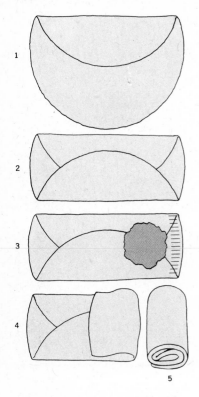

HOW TO SHAPE A CHIMICHANGO DULCE
Lay a 7-inch wheat tortilla flat and (1) turn down the top edge to a depth of about 2 inches. (2) Fold up the bottom 2 inches of the tortilla, overlapping the top and creating a band about 7 inches long and 3 inches wide. (3) Mound 2 tablespoons of filling an inch from one edge of the band. Spread a teaspoon of softened butter over the exposed edge at that end of the band, then (4) turn the buttered edge over the filling, covering it completely. (5) Starting at the filled end, roll the tortilla into a cylinder.

Assemble the *chimichangos* as shown in the diagrams above, using 2 tablespoons of the filling mixture and 1 tablespoon of the softened butter for each. (At this stage the *chimichangos dulces* may be wrapped in wax paper or foil and refrigerated for 2 or 3 hours.)

About half an hour before serving the *chimichangos,* preheat the oven to its lowest setting. Line a large jelly-roll pan with a double thickness of paper towels and place it in the center of the oven.

At the same time, pour vegetable oil into a deep fryer or large heavy saucepan to a depth of about 3 inches and heat the oil until it reaches a temperature of 375°.

Deep-fry two *chimichangos dulces* at a time, turning them about with a slotted spoon for 4 to 5 minutes, or until they are crisp and golden brown. As they brown, transfer them to the lined pan and keep them warm in the oven while you fry the rest.

Sprinkle the *chimichangos dulces* lightly with the confectioners' sugar, arrange them attractively on a large heated platter, and serve them while they are still hot.

Burritos and Chimichangos
ROLLED WHEAT TORTILLAS WITH BEAN-AND-POTATO FILLING

To make 8 rolled tortillas

BURRITOS
2 medium-sized boiling potatoes, peeled and quartered
2 cups freshly cooked or drained canned pinto, pink or kidney beans, rinsed in a sieve under cold running water if canned

½ cup water
2 canned green chilies (not the *jalapeño* variety), drained, halved, seeded and finely chopped
8 seven-inch wheat tortillas *(page 127)*

Drop the potatoes into enough boiling water to cover them completely and cook briskly, uncovered, until a potato quarter can be mashed against the side of the pan with the back of a fork. Drain the potatoes, then force them through a ricer or food mill set over a bowl. In a small skillet, bring the beans and water to a boil over moderate heat. Drain off the liquid and set it aside. With a fork, mash the beans to a coarse purée, beating in the reserved liquid by the spoonful if the beans seem dry. Add the beans to the potatoes, stir in the chilies, and taste for seasoning. Cover the bowl with foil to keep the filling mixture warm while you prepare the tortillas.

Place one tortilla in a heavy 10-inch skillet set over moderate heat, and turn it frequently with tongs for 30 seconds, or until it is soft. Spread ⅓ cup of the filling in a band 4 inches long and 1 inch wide across the center of the tortilla; then turn up the ends, fold one long side over the filling, and roll the tortilla into a cylinder. Repeat until all the tortillas are softened, filled and rolled. At this stage the tortillas are called *burritos*. Serve warm, accompanied if you like with red tomato taco sauce *(page 134)*.

ADDED INGREDIENT FOR
CHIMICHANGOS
Vegetable oil for deep frying

To make *chimichangos,* pour vegetable oil into a heavy 12-inch skillet to a depth of 1 inch, and heat the oil until it is very hot but not smoking. Fry the rolled tortillas two or three at a time, turning them with a slotted spoon, for about 2 minutes, until they are crisp and golden brown on all sides. As they brown, transfer the *chimichangos* to paper towels to drain.

Arrange the *chimichangos* on a heated platter and serve them hot, accompanied if you like by red tomato taco or *ancho* sauce *(pages 134 and 135)*.

Sopaipillas
DEEP-FRIED BREADS

To make 8 wedge-shaped or 12
  three-inch square *sopaipillas*

1½ cups unsifted flour
2 teaspoons double-acting baking
  powder
¾ teaspoon salt

2 tablespoons vegetable shortening,
  cut into ½-inch bits
½ cup lukewarm water (110° to
  115°)
Vegetable oil for deep frying

Combine the flour, baking powder and salt, and sift them into a deep bowl. Add the shortening bits, then, with your fingers, rub the flour and fat together until the mixture resembles flakes of coarse meal. Pour in the lukewarm water all at once and toss the dough together until it can be gathered into a compact ball.

On a lightly floured surface, knead the dough by pushing it down with the heels of your hands, pressing it forward and folding it back on itself. Knead for about 5 minutes, until the dough is smooth, shiny and elastic, then gather it into a ball, drape a kitchen towel over the top, and let the dough rest for about 15 minutes.

Meanwhile, pour vegetable oil into a deep fryer or large heavy saucepan to a depth of about 3 inches and heat the oil until it reaches a temperature of 400° on a deep-frying thermometer.

To make the wedge-shaped *sopaipillas* shown below, divide the dough in half and roll out each portion into a circle about 8 inches in diameter and ⅛ inch thick. With a pastry wheel or sharp knife, cut each circle into four equal wedges. To make square *sopaipillas,* roll out the dough into a rectangle about 12 inches long, 9 inches wide and ⅛ inch thick and cut the rectangle into 3-inch squares.

Two or three at a time, deep-fry the *sopaipillas* for about 3 minutes, turning them frequently with a slotted spoon. As they fry, the *sopaipillas* will puff up and brown. When they are crisp and golden on both sides, transfer them to paper towels to drain while you deep-fry the rest.

Serve the *sopaipillas* warm or at room temperature, accompanied with butter and honey.

Chiles Rellenos
BATTER-FRIED CHILIES WITH CHEESE FILLING

To serve 4 to 6

10 large fresh green *poblano* or *ancho* chilies or 10 canned green chilies (not the *jalapeño* variety)

½ pound sharp Cheddar cheese, sliced ¼ inch thick and cut into sticks 3 inches long and ¼ inch wide

⅓ cup finely chopped onions
Vegetable oil for deep frying
4 egg whites
¼ cup unsifted flour
¾ teaspoon double-acting baking powder
¼ teaspoon salt
4 egg yolks

If you are using the fresh chilies, preheat the broiler to its highest setting. Spread the chilies on a baking sheet and broil them 3 or 4 inches from the heat for 5 minutes, turning them so that they blister and darken on all sides. Wrap the chilies in a dampened kitchen towel and let them rest for a few minutes. Then rub them with the towels until the skins slip off. With a small sharp knife, cut all around the stem of each chili and pull out the stem and the seeds that cling to it. Discard the stems and seeds and set the chilies aside. If you are using canned chilies, drain and rinse them under cold running water. Cut a slit down the side of each chili. Spread the chilies flat and scrape away any seeds with a small knife.

Combine the cheese sticks and onions in a bowl and turn them about gently with a spoon until well mixed. Stuff the cheese-and-onion mixture into the fresh chilies through the stem openings, dividing the mixture evenly among them. To stuff the canned chilies, place equal portions of the cheese-and-onion mixture in the center of each chili. Fold the ends over the mixture and roll the chili around it. In either case, arrange the stuffed chilies on a plate or baking sheet and refrigerate them for about 1 hour before cooking.

Pour oil into a deep fryer or large heavy saucepan to a depth of about 3 inches and heat the oil until it reaches a temperature of 360° on a deep-frying thermometer. Preheat the oven to its lowest setting. Line a shallow baking pan with a double thickness of paper towels, and place the pan in the middle of the oven.

Prepare the batter coating for the chilies in the following manner: With a wire whisk or a rotary or electric beater, beat the egg whites until they are stiff enough to stand in unwavering peaks on the whisk or beater when it is lifted from the bowl. Combine the flour, baking powder and salt, and sift them together into a small bowl.

In a separate bowl with the same beater unwashed, beat the egg yolks for 2 or 3 minutes. When the yolks are thick, add the flour mixture and beat well. With a rubber spatula, scoop the egg whites over the yolks and fold them together gently but thoroughly.

Immerse one chili in the egg batter to coat it evenly, place the chili on

132

a saucer, and slide it carefully into the hot oil. Deep-fry two chilies at a time, turning them with a slotted spoon for 3 to 4 minutes, or until the batter puffs up and is golden brown. As they brown, transfer the chilies to the paper-lined pan and keep them warm in the oven.

Arrange the *chiles rellenos* attractively on a heated platter and serve at once while they are still hot.

Salsa Cruda
UNCOOKED VEGETABLE SAUCE

To make about 2 cups

A 1-pound can tomatoes, drained and finely chopped
A 4-ounce can Mexican green chilies (not the *jalapeño* variety), stemmed, seeded and finely chopped
½ cup finely chopped onions
1 tablespoon distilled white vinegar
1 teaspoon sugar

Combine the tomatoes, chilies, onions, vinegar and sugar in a bowl and stir until well mixed. Taste for seasoning. Let the *salsa cruda* rest at room temperature for about 30 minutes before serving. *Salsa cruda* is a traditional accompaniment to all-day beans *(page 113)* and may also be served with tacos or enchiladas.

Southwestern Pizza
To make one 15-inch pizza

1 tablespoon vegetable oil
A 15-inch wheat tortilla *(page 127)*
2 cups freshly grated longhorn or sharp Cheddar cheese
3 canned green chilies (not the *jalapeño* variety), drained, slit lengthwise in half, seeded and cut into ¼-inch-wide strips

Preheat the oven to 375°. With a pastry brush, spread the vegetable oil evenly over the bottom of a 15-inch pizza pan and place the wheat tortilla in the pan. Scatter the grated cheese over the tortilla. Then arrange the chilies on top in eight strips, radiating from the center like the spokes of a wheel.

Bake in the middle of the oven for 10 minutes, or until the cheese is melted and delicately browned. Serve at once, directly from the pan.

Jalapeño Chili Sauce

To make about ½ cup

A 4-ounce can pickled *jalapeño* chilies *(caution: see note, page 3)*

Drain the *jalapeño* chilies in a sieve set over a bowl, reserving all the brine. With a small sharp knife, cut off the stems. Slit the chilies lengthwise in half, scrape out the seeds with the point of the knife and chop the chilies into small pieces.

Place the chilies in the jar of an electric blender, pour in the reserved brine and blend at high speed for 30 seconds. Turn off the machine, scrape down the sides of the jar with a rubber spatula and blend again until the sauce is a smooth purée.

Jalapeño chili sauce may be served as an accompaniment to any kind of taco, enchilada or *tostada*. Caution your guests to use the sauce sparingly —*jalapeños* are one of the fieriest varieties of chilies.

Red Tomato Taco Sauce

To make 1½ to 2 cups

1 tablespoon lard	*pequín* chilies *(caution: see note, page 3)*
¼ cup finely chopped onions	1 teaspoon crumbled dried oregano
2 teaspoons finely chopped garlic	1 teaspoon sugar
2 cups canned tomato purée	1½ teaspoons salt
1 tablespoon finely crumbled seeded dried hot red chilies, preferably	1 teaspoon freshly ground black pepper

In a heavy 8- to 10-inch skillet, melt the lard over moderate heat until a drop of water flicked into it splutters and evaporates instantly. Add the onions and garlic and, stirring frequently, cook for about 5 minutes, or until they are soft and translucent but not brown. Stir in the tomato purée, chilies, oregano, sugar, salt and pepper, and bring to a boil over high heat. Reduce the heat to low, cover the skillet partially and simmer the sauce for 20 minutes.

Strain the sauce through a fine sieve set over a bowl, pressing down hard on the seasonings with the back of a spoon to extract all their juices before discarding the pulp. Serve at once. Or cool to room temperature, cover the bowl with plastic wrap and refrigerate until ready to serve. Tightly covered, the sauce can safely be kept for about a week.

Red tomato taco sauce is traditionally served as an accompaniment to any taco or *tostada*. Use it with care; taco sauce varies with the chilies that are used in it, but it is usually extremely hot.

Poor Man's Butter
AVOCADO-AND-TOMATO SAUCE

To make about 2 cups

2 large firm ripe avocados
2 tablespoons strained fresh lemon
  juice
2 large firm ripe tomatoes, peeled,
  seeded and cut into ¼-inch
  cubes *(see chile con queso, page 8)*

1 canned green chili (not the
  jalapeño variety), drained, seeded
  and finely chopped
3 tablespoons red wine vinegar
1 tablespoon vegetable oil
Salt

Cut the avocados in half. With the tip of a small knife, loosen the seeds and lift them out. Remove any brown tissuelike fibers clinging to the flesh. Starting at the narrow stem end, strip off the skin with your fingers or with a small knife. Cut the avocado into ¼-inch cubes and drop them into a bowl. Pour in the lemon juice and turn the cubes about gently with a spoon until they are evenly coated.

Add the tomatoes, chili, vinegar and oil, and toss together gently but thoroughly. Taste and season with salt, then let the sauce rest at room temperature for about 30 minutes before serving.

Poor man's butter is traditionally served as a spread for hot tortillas, and is also used as a filling for tacos or topping for *tostadas.*

Ancho Sauce
To make about 2 cups

12 dried *ancho* chilies *(caution: see
  note, page 3)*
2 cups boiling water
¼ cup tomato paste

1 teaspoon finely chopped garlic
1 teaspoon crumbled dried oregano
½ teaspoon ground cumin
½ teaspoon sugar
1½ teaspoons salt

Under cold running water, pull the stems off the *ancho* chilies, tear them in half and brush out their seeds. Tear the chilies into pieces, place them in a bowl and pour in the boiling water. The water should cover the chilies by at least 1 inch; if necessary, add more boiling water. Let the chilies soak for about 1 hour, then drain the soaking liquid into a bowl and reserve it. Force the chilies through a food mill set over a small heavy saucepan or rub them through a fine sieve with the back of a spoon.

Pour 1½ cups of the reserved soaking liquid into the chilies and mix well. Add the tomato paste, garlic, oregano, cumin, sugar and salt and, stirring constantly, bring to a boil over high heat. Reduce the heat to low and, stirring occasionally, simmer uncovered for 10 minutes, or until the sauce thickens enough to hold its shape lightly in a spoon. Taste for seasoning. Serve the sauce with tortillas, tacos or *tostadas.* Or transfer the sauce to a bowl, cool it to room temperature. Covered tightly and refrigerated, the sauce can safely be kept for about a week. Reheat it briefly before serving.

SOURDOUGH COOKERY

Sourdough Starter

Thousands of years before baking soda was discovered or commercial yeast became available, the ancient Egyptians made raised breads with sourdough, and sourdough "starters" have been bubbling away throughout the world ever since. In the United States, and particularly in the Great West, they impart a distinctive flavor and texture to waffles, pancakes and bread—most notably the great sourdough bread of San Francisco. Recipes for these foods and a pictorial guide to the preparation of sourdough bread are given on the following pages.

All these recipes must begin with the sourdough starter itself. Technically, the starter is a self-perpetuating leavening or fermenting agent composed of yeasts and bacteria, flour, water and sometimes sugar or other sweeteners. When added to a dough or batter, the starter makes the mixture rise. Part of the mixture is then set aside to become the starter for the next batch of dough or batter. Covered tightly and refrigerated, the starter may be stored for several weeks. If it is not used within that time, however, it must be freshened with additional flour and water (directions below). When used or freshened regularly, a starter keeps almost indefinitely—and its flavor improves with age.

¾ cup unsifted flour
½ cup warm water (90°)

1 package Sourdough Jack's starter mix *(Shopping Guide, page 150)*

Place the flour and warm water in a ceramic or glass bowl and beat them to a smooth paste with a wooden spoon. (Metal bowls should be avoided in all sourdough cooking. Sourdough is somewhat acid and will discolor some types of metal; more important, some metal bowls may impart an unpleasant taste to the final product.)

Add the starter mix to the bowl and stir until the ingredients are well blended. Using a rubber spatula, scrape the mixture into a pint jar equipped with a tightly fitting lid. Cover the jar securely and set it aside in a warm, draft-free place (such as an unlighted oven) for 48 hours. The mixture will ferment and bubble.

Use the starter at once, or refrigerate it in the jar. It can safely be kept for 2 or 3 weeks. If not used within that time, freshen the starter in the following fashion: Remove the jar from the refrigerator and let the starter warm to room temperature. Scrape the mixture into a deep bowl, stir in 1 cup of warm (90°) water and then add 1 cup of flour. Cover the bowl tightly with plastic wrap and set the starter aside in a warm (80°), draft-free place for about 1 hour, or until fermentation begins and the mixture bubbles. Ladle 1 cup of the starter into the pint jar, cover tightly and refrigerate. Discard the starter remaining in the bowl.

This freshening procedure must be repeated every 2 or 3 weeks throughout the life of the starter unless the starter is used with regularity. As it stands, the starter will separate and liquid will rise to the top. Before using or freshening the starter, stir it briefly to recombine it; do not pour off the surface liquid.

If at any time the starter does not begin to ferment when fresh flour and water are added, the starter is dead and must be discarded.

Sourdough Waffles

To make four 11-by-6-inch waffles

1 cup sourdough starter (opposite)
2 cups warm water (90°)
2½ cups unsifted flour
1 egg, lightly beaten

¼ cup vegetable oil
½ cup dry milk solids
2 tablespoons sugar
1 teaspoon baking soda
1 teaspoon salt

With a rubber spatula, scrape the starter into a deep ceramic or glass bowl. Give it a quick stir to recombine its ingredients, then add the warm water and stir the mixture to a paste. Stir in the flour, about ½ cup at a time. Cover the bowl tightly with plastic wrap and set the mixture aside in a warm, draft-free place (such as an unlighted oven) for 12 hours. (If the mixture has not bubbled at the end of this time, the starter was dead and the mixture must be discarded.) You should have about 4 cups of sourdough mixture.

Before preparing the waffles, ladle 1 cup of the mixture into a pint jar to serve as a starter for future sourdough cooking. Cover the jar tightly with its lid and refrigerate the starter until you are ready to use it. Unless the starter is used within 2 or 3 weeks, freshen it as described above.

With a wire whisk, beat the egg and vegetable oil into the 3 cups of sourdough mixture remaining in the bowl to form a sourdough batter. Combine the dry milk solids, sugar, baking soda and salt in a small sifter,

Continued on next page

sprinkle them directly over the batter and whisk all of the ingredients together gently but thoroughly.

Following the manufacturer's directions, preheat an 11-by-6-inch waffle iron to moderate. Pour 1½ cups of the batter into the center of the hot waffle iron, reduce the heat to moderately low and close the iron. Bake for 5 minutes, or until the steaming stops and the waffle is golden brown on both sides. (You can peek at the waffle to check it after 3 minutes, but do not open the cover earlier or the waffle may stick to the grid.)

Serve the sourdough waffles at once, accompanied by butter and maple syrup, honey or jam.

Sourdough Pancakes

To make 25 to 30 two-inch
    pancakes

	½ cup dry milk solids
1 cup sourdough starter *(page 136)*	2 tablespoons sugar
2 cups warm water (90°)	1 teaspoon baking soda
2½ cups unsifted flour	1 teaspoon salt
1 egg, lightly beaten	4 to 6 tablespoons butter, melted
2 tablespoons vegetable oil	and cooled

With a rubber spatula, scrape the sourdough starter into a deep ceramic or glass bowl and give it a quick stir to recombine its ingredients. Add the warm water and stir the mixture to a smooth paste. Stir in the flour about ½ cup at a time. Then cover the bowl tightly with plastic wrap and set the sourdough mixture in a warm, draft-free place (such as an unlighted oven) for 12 hours. (If the mixture has not bubbled at the end of this time, the starter was dead and the mixture must be discarded.) You should have about 4 cups of sourdough mixture.

Before preparing the pancakes, ladle 1 cup of the mixture into a 1-pint jar to serve as a starter for future sourdough cooking. Cover the jar tightly with its lid and refrigerate the starter until ready to use. Unless the starter is used within 2 or 3 weeks, freshen it as described on page 137.

With a wire whisk, beat the egg and vegetable oil into the 3 cups of sourdough mixture remaining in the bowl to form a batter. Combine the dry milk solids, sugar, baking soda and salt in a sifter, sprinkle them over the batter and whisk the ingredients together gently but thoroughly.

Warm a large heavy griddle over moderate heat until a drop of water flicked onto it splutters and evaporates instantly. Grease the griddle lightly with a pastry brush dipped in the melted butter.

Fry five or six pancakes at a time, leaving enough space between them so that they can spread into 2-inch rounds. For each pancake, pour about 2 tablespoons of the batter onto the griddle and fry for about a minute until small, scattered bubbles have formed and begin to break on the surface. Immediately, turn the pancake with a wide metal spatula and cook for a minute, until the bottom is golden brown.

Stack the finished pancakes on a heated plate. Then repeat the procedure, brushing the griddle with melted butter when necessary, until all the sourdough pancakes are cooked. Serve the pancakes at once, accompanied by butter and maple syrup, honey or jam.

San Francisco Sourdough Bread

This recipe was developed by amateur chef Joseph A. Flaherty, a resident of Port Washington, New York, but a regular visitor to California, who also demonstrates the procedure on the following pages. Baking this bread is no casual undertaking. The first batch takes over 3 days from start to finish, and successive batches require about 18 hours each.

For optimum results, the cook must improvise a counterpart to a baker's brick hearth oven by setting building bricks on the oven shelves; the cook should also make or purchase "proofing," or rising, trays, construct or improvise a proofing box in which the bread can rise, and purchase or make baker's "peels," or shovels, to transfer the bread to the oven. (These devices are described more fully in the instructions below and illustrated in the pictures.) For information about purchasing trays, peels and flour, see the Shopping Guide, page 150. The quantities of dough specified must also be weighed carefully on kitchen scales for best results.

This sourdough bread warrants the efforts expended. It is high in quality, and the loaves have the distinctive flavor, the springy texture, and the thick crisp crusts of their San Francisco prototype. This recipe may be doubled—if you have the strength to knead 6 pounds of dough.

To make three 1-pound long loaves
    or two 1½-pound round loaves

BASIC SOURDOUGH BREAD STARTER	hard-wheat bread flour,
1 cup sourdough starter *(page 136)*	preferably unbleached
¾ cup plus 2 tablespoons unsifted	1 teaspoon butter, softened

BASIC SOURDOUGH BREAD STARTER: Place the sourdough starter in a deep glass or ceramic mixing bowl, add 2 or 3 tablespoons of flour, and stir them together vigorously with a large wooden spoon. Repeat four or five more times until you have added ¾ cup of flour, and beat well after

Continued on next page   139

each addition. Continue to stir until the dough can be gathered into a stiff, though somewhat rough, ball.

Spread the remaining 2 tablespoons of flour on a breadboard, set the ball on top of it and knead—pressing the dough down, pushing it forward and folding it back on itself. Repeat for 10 minutes, until the dough is smooth and can be stretched about 3 inches without breaking.

Let the dough rest on the breadboard for about 5 minutes. Meanwhile, wash the mixing bowl, and with a pastry brush spread the inside with the 1 teaspoon of softened butter. Place the dough in the bowl and turn it about to butter the entire surface of the dough. Cover the bowl tightly with plastic wrap and set the dough aside in a warm (80°), draft-free place (such as an unlighted oven) for 8 hours. In this time the starter will double or even triple in volume and will be fully developed.

The bread starter will weigh about 11 ounces. It can be used immediately, or all or part of the starter can be punched down and stored in a tightly covered nonmetallic container in the refrigerator until the next batch of bread is to be baked. The starter can be held in this state in the refrigerator for up to one month, but do not freeze it. It should be freshened each time bread is baked and will last for years if freshened regularly.

SOURDOUGH STARTER SPONGE

4 ounces basic sourdough bread
    starter *(page 139)*
¼ cup warm water (90°)

1 cup unsifted hard-wheat bread
    flour, preferably unbleached
1 teaspoon butter, softened

SOURDOUGH STARTER SPONGE: For the second, and each successive batch of sourdough bread, a starter "sponge" must be set the night before and allowed to ferment and develop for 8 to 10 hours. In baking, a sponge is rising dough; it gets its name from its cellular, "spongy" texture. In this instance, the sponge is a small amount of rising dough that is used as the base and leavening agent for the bread.

To prepare the sponge, cut off 4 ounces of the basic starter and stretch it with your hands five or six times. Break it into four small pieces and drop them into ¼ cup of warm (90°) water in a glass or ceramic mixing bowl. Add ¼ cup of flour and stir together vigorously with a large wooden spoon. Repeat until you have added ¾ cup of flour and beat well after each addition. Continue to stir the dough until it can be gathered into a stiff, somewhat rough, ball.

Spread 2 tablespoons of flour smoothly on a large breadboard. Set the ball on top of it and knead—pressing the dough down with the heels of your hands, pushing it forward 6 to 8 inches, and folding it back on itself. As you knead, gradually incorporate 2 tablespoons more flour as necessary, to prevent the dough from sticking to the board. Knead the dough for 5 to 10 minutes, until it is smooth and elastic enough for one edge to be stretched about 3 inches without breaking *(photograph, page 144)*.

Let the dough rest on the breadboard for 5 minutes. Meanwhile, wash the mixing bowl, and with a pastry brush spread the inside with 1 teaspoon of softened butter. Place the dough in the bowl and turn it about to butter the entire surface. Cover the bowl tightly with plastic wrap and set it aside in a warm (80°), draft-free place for 8 to 10 hours.

The next morning, the sponge will have doubled or tripled in bulk. Mix the sourdough bread dough starting with this fully developed starter sponge. The starter sponge will weigh about 11 ounces.

SOURDOUGH BREAD DOUGH	1 tablespoon salt
5 ounces basic sourdough starter	1 teaspoon butter, softened
or starter sponge	¼ to ⅓ cup rice flour
2 cups warm water (90°)	2 to 3 tablespoons yellow cornmeal
7 cups unsifted hard-wheat bread	1 egg white lightly beaten with
flour, preferably unbleached	2 tablespoons water

SOURDOUGH BREAD DOUGH: Cut off 5 ounces of fully developed basic sourdough bread starter or starter sponge. (Refrigerate the remaining starter or sponge in a tightly covered nonmetallic container to serve as starter for the next batch.) Pour 2 cups of warm (90°) water into a heavy 6-quart ceramic mixing bowl. Break the 5 ounces of starter or sponge into 12 small pieces, dropping them into the water as you proceed.

Stirring the mixture constantly with a large wooden spoon, slowly sprinkle in ½ cup of flour. Add 1 level tablespoon of salt. (Be precise; even a small amount of extra salt will severely inhibit the rising power of the sourdough.) Then add 5½ cups more flour, ½ cup at a time, mixing well with your hands after each addition. Continue to mix until the dough can be gathered into a rough, though somewhat sticky, ball. Spread 2 tablespoons of the remaining cup of flour on a breadboard and reserve the rest. Place the dough on the board and knead—pushing it down, pressing it forward 6 to 8 inches and folding it back on itself. As you knead, gradually incorporate flour from the reserved cup, sprinkling it over and under the dough by the tablespoonful and adding only as much as you need to make a nonsticky dough.

Continue kneading vigorously for at least 20 minutes, until the dough is smooth, satiny and elastic. This long kneading time is important to expand the gluten in the flour so that the loaves will hold their shape throughout the long proofing, or rising, process.

Let the dough rest for 5 minutes while you clean the bowl. Brush the bowl with 1 teaspoon of softened butter. Place the dough in the bowl and turn it about to butter the entire surface. Cover the bowl tightly with plastic wrap and set it in a warm (80°), draft-free place for one hour.

The sourdough will *not* rise significantly during this first hour. It

Continued on next page 141

should not increase much in volume at this point because natural sourdough yeast will not maintain its rising action through multiple proofings.

PREPARING THE OVEN: Arrange the racks of your oven so that one is about 4 inches from the bottom floor and a second about 4 inches from the top. Cover each rack with common building bricks with the flat side up—each rack should hold about 8 to 10 bricks. Set the oven regulator to 400° and preheat the bricks. It may take up to 3 hours for the bricks to reach this temperature. Bricks are essential to hold the oven temperature even and to give the loaves the intense, even heat necessary for them to attain the proper shape at the onset of the baking.

SHAPING AND PROOFING THE LOAVES: Return the dough to the breadboard and with a large sharp knife cut off 2 ounces and add them to the refrigerated starter to refresh it. Then cut the dough in half if you wish to make round loaves, or into thirds for long loaves. Weigh each piece. The halves should each weigh about 1½ pounds; the thirds should each weigh about 1 pound. Any extra dough should be added to the refrigerated starter; if there is too much for the container, discard the excess.

Shape each piece of dough into a smooth ball. Sprinkle 1 tablespoon of rice flour on the breadboard and set the balls of dough on it, cover them with plastic wrap, and let them rest for 15 minutes.

San Francisco sourdough bread is not baked in pans and tends to flatten and lose its shape unless properly formed and proofed. The long loaves are proofed on special divided trays like the one shown on page 147.

The proofing tray shown on page 147 was made from a piece of plywood 14 inches wide and 20 inches long to which six 1-by-1-by-20-inch wood strips have been nailed 1½ inches apart. You can make similar trays from plywood or fiberboard. Metal proofing trays are available ready-made (Shopping Guide, page 150).

The round loaves are proofed on a breadboard large enough to hold them. Remember that they will expand as they rise, so allow ample space between the loaves. Before shaping the dough into loaves, spread a pastry cloth or a heavy linen towel over the appropriate proofing tray and sprinkle the cloth evenly with 2 to 3 tablespoons of rice flour.

Following the directions on pages 146 and 147, shape the balls of dough into cylindrical or round loaves. Arrange the loaves on the cloth-lined proofing trays and set them aside in a warm (80°), draft-free place next to a pan of warm water. Cover the trays and pan with an inverted cardboard box. High humidity is essential to proper proofing. Without it, the loaves may dry out or develop tough crusts.

To control the temperature and humidity more exactly, the dough should be allowed to rise, or "proof," in a closed box with an interior temperature of 80° and a relative humidity of 90 per cent. The box shown on page 148 was made from a heavy shipping crate, outfitted with a 25-watt

light for heat and a pan of warm (90°) water for moisture. A simple ther-
mometer and a humidity indicator make it possible to check and maintain
optimum proofing conditions.

The loaves must rise slowly to allow fermentation to develop the sour flavor so typical of sourdough bread. The proofing will take 3 to 4 hours at 80°. After 3½ hours, when the loaves have at least doubled in volume, poke a hole about ½ inch deep into the side of a loaf with your fingertip. If the dough is properly proofed, the loaf will slowly return to its original shape. (If the dough does not spring back, the loaves are over-proofing and should be baked at once.)

BAKING THE BREAD: About 10 minutes before baking the bread, place a shallow pan on the hot floor of the oven, or, if the oven is electric, directly on top of the bottom heating coil. Pour boiling water into the pan and let the steam saturate the oven. Remove the proofing trays from the proofing box and let the loaves rest at room temperature for 5 minutes. Just before baking, increase the oven temperature to 425° and add more boiling water to the pan. Steam is essential for the baking.

Sprinkle a round baker's peel slightly larger than each round loaf with 1 tablespoon of the cornmeal. Slip both hands gently under one loaf and carefully lift it onto the peel. With a single-edge razor blade or the razor-edged device shown on page 149, cut four intersecting lines in a square pattern on top of each round loaf as shown.

Slide the peel into the oven across the bricks and quickly jerk it out from under the loaf. Sprinkle the peel again with 1 tablespoon of cornmeal and repeat the procedure with the second round loaf.

To transfer a long loaf from the proofing tray, you will need two peels, each 18 inches long and about 5 inches wide. Sprinkle one of the peels with 1 tablespoon of cornmeal and dust the other lightly with rice flour. Hold the peel covered with rice flour next to the loaf, as shown on page 148. Tip the loaf onto the peel by lifting one edge of the pastry cloth and then turn the loaf over onto the cornmeal-covered peel.

With a razor blade, cut four 3-inch-long overlapping diagonal slashes in the top of each loaf as shown on page 149. Slide the peel lengthwise into the oven directly over the bricks and quickly jerk it back out from under the loaf so that the bread bakes directly on the bricks. Repeat the procedure until all of the loaves are in the oven, sprinkling the peels with 1 tablespoon of cornmeal and 1 tablespoon of rice flour each time.

Bake the loaves for 15 minutes, then lower the oven temperature to 375° and continue baking for 15 minutes longer. Slide the loaves out of the oven on a peel, one at a time, and brush the tops lightly with the mixture of egg white and water. Bake the loaves for about 10 minutes longer, or until the crusts are crisp and a rich golden-brown color and the loaves sound hollow when thumped on the bottom. Use the peels to remove the bread from the oven and transfer the loaves to wire racks to cool.

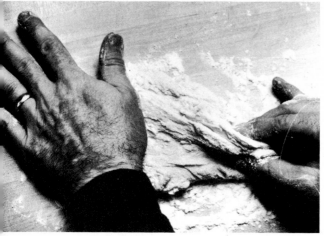

TEXTURE BEGINS WITH THE BREAD STARTER
To expand the gluten in the flour, make the dough elastic and ensure a smooth-textured loaf, the sourdough bread starter *(page 139)* must be well kneaded. (1) Holding an edge of the dough in one hand, press the dough flat and push it forward about 6 inches with the heel of your other hand. Then fold the dough back on itself. (2) Repeat for 10 minutes, until the dough can stretch 3 inches without breaking.

3   4   5

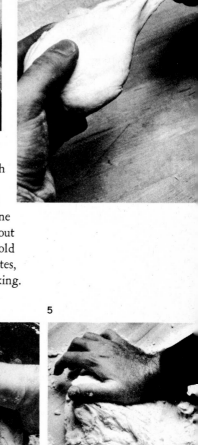

KNEADING TO MAKE THE BREAD DOUGH STRONG AND LIGHT
After the starter doubles in volume, (3) pour warm water into a bowl and drop in the starter, a bit at a time. (4) Add salt and flour *(see recipe for proportions)* and mix with your hands until you can gather the dough into a ball. (5) Place the dough on a board and knead vigorously for 20 minutes.

A San Francisco Sourdough Bread You Can Make in Your Own Kitchen

The ingredients for San Francisco sourdough bread are few: sourdough starter, hard-wheat bread flour (preferably unbleached), warm water and salt. A complete recipe for the bread appears on page 139, but its success depends upon attention to detail. The starter must be active and bubbly. Only bread flour milled with hard wheat will produce a dough strong enough to keep its shape and encapsulate the gases that ensure a light-textured crumb. The water must be 90°: warmer water may kill the yeast in the starter; colder water will retard or prevent the growth of the yeast. Even the salt must be measured precisely—too much can slow or stop the rising process. Once mixed, the dough must be kneaded long and vigorously to develop elasticity. After it rises (or is proofed), the dough must be shaped carefully and the loaves treated gingerly. The pictures on these and the following pages will help you to master the techniques, from the first kneading to the finished loaf.

When the dough is fully kneaded, it will appear smooth and satiny. Place it in a buttered bowl, cover tightly and set the dough in a warm, draft-free place for an hour. Do not allow the dough to double in volume: overrising at this stage will exhaust the leavening power of the sourdough. Cut the dough in half if you plan to make round loaves *(left)*, into thirds for long loaves. The cut surfaces will appear porous, as shown at left.

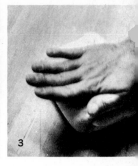

1

2

3

FIRST STEPS IN SHAPING A SOURDOUGH LOAF

For each loaf, place a half or third of the dough on an unfloured surface and, with your hands, pound it into a flat round about ½ inch thick. (1) Fold down the top third of the round and pound it hard. (2) Then turn the bottom third up to overlap the top and pound again. (3) Fold both ends into the middle, overlapping them to make a square, and pound after each fold.

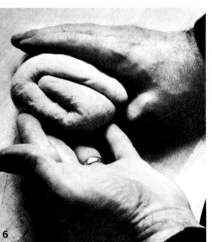

6

7

8

SHAPING A LONG SOURDOUGH LOAF

(6) Place the square of dough *(step 3, above)* on the board with one folded end toward you and (7), starting with the folded end, roll the square into a tight cylinder. (8) Turn the dough seam side down and, with your hands in the center, roll it back and forth. Gradually move your hands to the ends to elongate the loaf. Repeat, pressing firmly to force out air bubbles, until (9) the loaf is about 17 inches long and 1½ inches in diameter and tapers at both ends.

SHAPING A ROUND SOURDOUGH LOAF
(4) Hold the square of dough seam side down and, with both hands, turn the ends under. (5) Smooth down the top and sides, and turn the dough between your hands for a minute or two, pressing firmly to form a tight, even ball with all the rough edges securely tucked beneath it. Place the loaf gently on a breadboard covered with a pastry cloth sprinkled with rice flour.

Shaped long loaves are set out to rise, or "proof," on a special tray (the one shown is homemade) with low ridges to support the sides of the loaves. Round loaves are proofed on a flat board. Either tray should be draped with a pastry cloth dusted with rice flour.

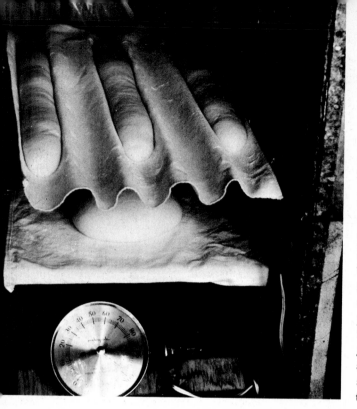

PROOFING THE LOAVES
Shaped sourdough loaves
(left) must rise, or proof,
for 4 hours in a draft-free
place with a temperature of
80° and a relative
humidity of 90 per cent.
Although you can
improvise with a carton,
the ideal method is to place
the trays in an airtight
proofing box. (Joseph
Flaherty, who developed
the recipe on page 139,
made the box, shown
opened here, from a
packing crate.) With a
thermometer, a humidity
gauge, a 25-watt light bulb
and a pan of warm water,
a home baker can control
temperature and humidity.

BAKING LONG LOAVES
To slide the loaves into the oven,
you need two long baker's "peels,"
or shovels. Sprinkle one peel with
rice flour, the other with cornmeal.
(1) Place the peel coated with rice
flour at one side of a long loaf and
lift the pastry cloth to turn the loaf
over onto the peel. Set the meal-
covered peel next to the loaf and
tip the loaf upside down onto it.
(2) Slit the loaf with four 3-inch-
long gashes, using a single-edged
razor blade or a double-edged blade
fitted onto the end of a popsicle
stick. Slide the loaf into the oven.
(3) Bake for 30 minutes, brush
with a mixture of egg white and
water and bake 10 minutes more.

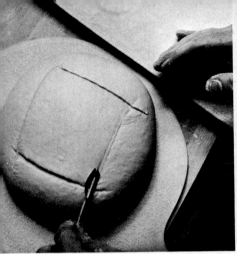

BAKING ROUND LOAVES

Pick up one loaf at a time, and set it on a round, cornmeal-covered baker's peel, or shovel. Cut four intersecting slits in the top *(above)* and slide the loaf into the oven. After 30 minutes, brush each loaf with a mixture of egg white and water *(right)* for the final baking.

2

3

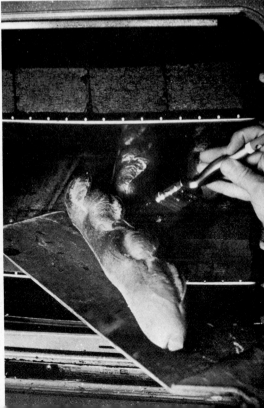

Sources for Foods and Utensils

Mexican-American Supplies

Taco fryers, tortilla presses, dried hot peppers, canned green and red chilies, canned *jalapeño* chilies, canned *tomatitos, masa harina, chorizo* sausage and frozen tortillas can be obtained from a number of sources, listed by state and city. Because policies differ and managements change, check with the store nearest you to determine what it has in stock, the current prices, and how best to order the items that interest you. Not all stores have every item.

TACO FRYER *(page 121)*:
Casa Molina Mfg. Co.
6225 East Speedway Blvd.
Tucson, Arizona 85716

The foods mentioned above can be obtained from the following sources. Stores marked with an asterisk also carry tortilla presses.

Arizona
El Molino
117 South 22nd St.
Phoenix 85034

Sasabe Store
P.O. Box 7
Sasabe 85633

Best Supermarket
55555 East 5th St.
Tucson 85711

Bullards*
7113 North Oracle Rd.
Tucson 85704

Santa Cruz Chili and Spice Co.
P.O. Box 177
Tumacacori 85640

California
Mercado La Tepiquena
2030 Del Paso Blvd.
North Sacramento 95815

La Victoria Foods, Inc.
9200 West Whitmore St.
Rosemead 91770

Casa Lucas Market*
2934-24th St.
San Francisco 94110

Florida
Alamo Tortilla Factory
Kirk Plaza
Suite 9-B
Titusville 32780

Iowa
Nelson's Meat Market
3201 1st Ave., SE
Cedar Rapids 52403

Swiss Colony*
Lindale Plaza
Cedar Rapids 52403

Michigan
La Paloma
2620 Bagley St.
Detroit 48216

Minnesota
La Casa Coronado Restaurant*
23 North 6th St.
Minneapolis 55403

Missouri
Heidi's Around the World Food
    Shop
1149 South Brentwood
St. Louis 63117

New York
Casa Moneo Spanish Imports*
210 West 14th St.
New York 10011

Pennsylvania
Kaufmann's Department Store
Epicure Shop
5th Ave. & Smithfield St.
Pittsburgh 15219

Stamcolis Bros. Grocery
2020 Penn Ave.
Pittsburgh 15222

Texas
Caliente Chili Co.
P.O. Box 1444
Austin 78767
(For prepared "Two-Alarm"
dried chili mix only.)

Adobe House*
127 Payne St.
Dallas 75207

Simon David Grocery Store
711 Inwood Rd.
Dallas 75209

Ashley's, Inc.
6590 Montana Ave.
El Paso 79925

Gebhardt Mexican Foods Co.
P.O. Box 7130, Station A
San Antonio 78207

Los Cocos Products*
202 Produce Row
San Antonio 78207

Washington
El Ranchito*
P.O. Box 717
Zillah 98953

Bread and Baking Supplies

DRIED SOURDOUGH STARTER:
Sourdough Jack's Kitchen
2901 Clement St.
San Francisco, Calif. 94121

UNBLEACHED HARD-WHEAT FI
El Molino Mills
P.O. Box 2025
Alhambra, Calif. 91803

Carolyn Foods, Inc.
P.O. Box 311
Ithaca, N.Y. 14850

Great Valley Mills
Quakertown, Pa. 18951

BAKING AND PROOFING TRAYS
Argonaut House
2901 Clement St.
San Francisco, Calif. 94121

ROSE TUBES AND FLOWER NAI
Mail Order Sales
Wilton Enterprises, Inc.
933 West 115th St.
Chicago, Ill. 60643

Recipe Index

NOTE: Size, weight and material are specified for pans in the recipes because they affect cooking results. A pan should be just large enough to hold its contents comfortably. Heavy pans heat slowly and cook food at a constant rate. Aluminum and cast iron conduct heat well but may discolor foods that are made with egg yolks, wine, vinegar or lemon. Enamelware is a fairly poor conductor of heat. Many recipes recommend stainless steel or enameled cast iron, which do not have these faults.

Introductory Notes
How to handle hot chilies 3
Techniques for home canning 2

Appetizers and First Courses
Angelenos (angels on horseback,
  California style) 8
Caraway twists 12
Cheese balls 14
Chile con queso (cheese-and-green-chili
  dip) 8
Cold boiled artichokes with
  tuna mayonnaise 6
Crab-olive spread 9
Guacamole with chilies 7
Huevos Monterey (tortillas with artichokes
  and eggs) 5
Texas broiled shrimp 4
Texas caviar (pickled black-eyed peas) 11
Turcos (tiny spiced-beef turnovers) 10
Zucchini Victor 13

Soups
Artichoke soup 16
Bowl of the Wife of Kit Carson 18
Dill soup 21
Menudo (spicy tripe-and-pig's-feet
  soup) 20
Mormon split-pea soup 19
Sopa de albóndigas (spiced meatball
  soup) 15

Salads and Dressings
Apricot-cream dressing 28
Beer coleslaw 24
Caviar-potato salad 22
Ginger-ale salad 23
Lime-gelatin salad 26
Mayonnaise 29
Molded horseradish salad 24
Poppy-seed dressing 27
Spinach-and-bacon salad 25
Strawberry-and-sour-cream dressing 27
Yoghurt-and-honey dressing 28

Vegetables and Garnishes
Basque sheepherders' potatoes 30
Calabacitas agrias y dulces (sweet-and-sour
  squash) 35
Cebollas rellenas (baked onions with
  meat-and-chili stuffing) 34
Chili jelly 42
Colache (vegetable stew) 37
Coliflor fria (cold spiced cauliflower
  salad) 39
Deep-fried okra 38
Eggplant-banana casserole 36
Ginger fruit kabobs 41
Hashed brown potatoes 33
Okra and tomatoes 38
Pinto beans 40
Stuffed baked potatoes with cheese 32
Stuffed baked potatoes with sour cream 31
Trappers' fruit 40

Seafood
Abalone steaks 44
Cioppino 54
Crab Louis 45
Fillet of rex sole Santa Monica 51
Minted trout 53
Pan-fried trout 52
San Francisco fried trout 52
Sand dab or rex sole *en papillote* 50
Shrimp and chilies with sherry sauce 43
Sole-and-crab mousse with shrimp sauce 46
Stuffed flounder 48

Poultry and Game Birds
Chicken-*jalapeño* pancakes 58
Chicken Raphael Weill 60
Grapefruit duck 56
Hearst Ranch squab 65
Lemon chicken 57
Quail in lemon-wine sauce 62
Spit-roasted quail with grapes 63
Spit-roasted wild ducks with olives 64
Turkey chili 61

Meats

Barbecued spareribs with red sauce 72
Broiled ham steak with canteloupe 66
Carne Santa Fe (spiced braised beef) 71
Charcoal-broiled T-bone or
    porterhouse steak 78
Chuletas de carnero con piñones (lamb chops
    with pine nuts) 69
Cowboy short ribs with
    cornmeal dumplings 76
Fresh red chili sauce 73
Lamb and broccoli St. Francis 70
√ Lamb and limas 68
Olive beef stew 78
Rabbit in tarragon cream gravy 79
Red pork chili 73
Texas chili con carne 74
Vineyard leg of lamb 67
Zuñi green-chili stew 75

Breads

Cowboy soda biscuits 85
Date, pecan and orange bread 80
Monkey bread 84
Mormon johnnycake 86
Mormon rye bread 82
Navajo fry bread 83
Wheat-germ hamburger buns 81

Mexican-American Dishes

All-day beans 113
Ancho sauce 135
Beef tacos 120
Bocoles (corn-flour-and-bean cakes) 115
Burritos and chimichangos (rolled filled wheat
    tortillas) 130
Chicken tostadas (fried tortillas
    with topping) 119
Chiles rellenos (batter-fried chilies
    with cheese) 132
Chimichangos dulces (deep-fried fruit-filled
    tortillas) 128
Chorizo flautas (rolled tortillas with
    sausage filling) 122
Corn tortillas 118
Enchiladas de Jocoque (filled
    tortillas) 124
Green-chili sauce 126
Green corn tamales 116
Jalapeño chili sauce 134
Poor man's butter (avocado-and-tomato
    sauce) 135
Red tomato taco sauce 134
Refried beans 114
Salsa cruda (uncooked vegetable
    sauce) 133
Sopaipillas (deep-fried breads) 131
Southwestern pizza 133
Stacked cheese enchiladas, New Mexico
    style 126
Tostaditas (deep-fried corn chips) 122
Wheat tortillas 127

Desserts and Pastries

Almond-topped cookies 108
Bizcochuelos (licorice cookies) 110
Buttermilk poundcake 102
C Lazy U doughnuts 111
Fig squares 106
German's chocolate cake with
    coconut frosting 100
Glass cookies 108
Glazed oranges 87
Grapefruit cake with cream-cheese icing 94
Houston gingerbread 99
Lalla Rookh 88
Lemon bars 112
Lime chiffon pie 92
Lollies 107
Oatmeal cookies 109
Osgood pie 91
Pecan cake 93
Pecan drops 106
Pecan-stuffed date cookies 104
Pecan tassies 105
Postre borracho ("drunken" cake) 103
San Antonio fruit ice cream 89
Sheath cake 98
Short-crust pastry 90

Sourdough Cookery

San Francisco sourdough bread 139
Sourdough pancakes 138
Sourdough starter 136
Sourdough waffles 137

Photographs on pages 49 and 96 by Mark Kauffman; photographs on page 121 by Richard Henry. All illustrations are by Albert Sherman.